INTO THE JAWS OF DEATH

PRIVATE JACK O'BRIEN

1st WORLD
LIBRARY
Literary Society

Into the Jaws of Death

Jack O'Brien

© 1st World Library, 2007
PO Box 2211
Fairfield, IA 52556
www.1stworldlibrary.com
First Edition

LCCN: 2007927838

Softcover ISBN: 978-1-4218-4549-4
Hardcover ISBN: 978-1-4218-4465-7
eBook ISBN: 978-1-4218-4633-0

Purchase *"Into the Jaws of Death"*
as a traditional bound book at:
www.1stWorldLibrary.com/purchase.asp?ISBN= 978-1-4218-4549-4

1st World Library is a literary, educational organization
dedicated to:

- Creating a free internet library of downloadable ebooks

- Hosting writing competitions and offering book publishing
scholarships.

Interested in more 1st World Library books? contact:
literacy@1stworldlibrary.com
Check us out at: www.1stworldlibrary.com

1st World Library Literary Society

Giving Back to the World

"If you want to work on the core problem, it's early school literacy."

- James Barksdale, former CEO of Netscape

"No skill is more crucial to the future of a child, or to a democratic and prosperous society, than literacy."

- Los Angeles Times

"Literacy... means far more than learning how to read and write... The aim is to transmit... knowledge and promote social participation."

- UNESCO

"Literacy is not a luxury, it is a right and a responsibility. If our world is to meet the challenges of the twenty-first century we must harness the energy and creativity of all our citizens."

- President Bill Clinton

"Parents should be encouraged to read to their children, and teachers should be equipped with all available techniques for teaching literacy, so the varying needs and capacities of individual kids can be taken into account."

- Hugh Mackay

TO LIEUT.-COLONEL J. F. L. EMBURY
AND THE OFFICERS AND MEN OF THE 28TH
NORTHWEST BATTALION,
I RESPECTFULLY DEDICATE THIS BOOK

CONTENTS

FOREWORD

Having been asked by the Author of this Book, No. 73,194 Private Jack O'Brien of the 28th Northwest Battalion, to write a few words as an introduction to the story which he is placing before the public, it gives me much pleasure to do so.

The 6th Canadian Infantry Brigade raised and organized from the four western provinces of Canada has done its share and at the time of writing it is still doing its share in the field against the common enemy. The 28th Northwest Battalion, originally under the Command of Lieut.-Col. J. F. L. Embury, C.M.G., has taken its share in all the engagements in which the 6th Canadian Infantry Brigade took part, including St. Eloi, Hooge, three engagements on the Somme, 15th September, 26th September, and 1st October, 1916, as well as the general engagements of Vimy Ridge, Fresnoy, Lens on the 21st August, 1917, and Passchendaele, and in each of these engagements, alongside the remaining Battalions of the Brigade—namely, the 27th City of Winnipeg Battalion, 29th Vancouver Battalion, and the 31st Alberta Battalion—never failed in gaining all of the objectives which had been set for the Brigade to carry. Whenever any special raids to obtain information and identifications were called for, the 28th Northwest Battalion invariably volunteered for such duty, and their efforts were always crowned with success. In fact the record of the

Brigade throughout the campaign has been an outstanding one, and the various matters which Private Jack O'Brien refers to in his book will be of the greatest interest to all members of the Brigade, past and present, as well as to the general public in Western Canada.

The feat accomplished by this young soldier in escaping from the Germans, whilst held as a prisoner of war, is in itself worthy of special notice and he was only successful in his third attempt. His conduct and record in the field is one to be proud of, and I have no hesitation in introducing him to the readers of his most interesting book. As a soldier he has done his duty and is deserving of every support in the circulation of his war story.

H. D. B. KETCHEN,

Brig.-Gen. comm'd'g 6th Can. Inf. Brig.

10th April, 1918

CHAPTER I

"Well, boy, how did you do it?" "What are the prison camps like?" "Are the Germans as cruel as they are painted?" These are the questions that I have been asked thousands of times since coming home. I have answered them from scores of platforms, for all kinds of Red Cross organizations; and now I have been persuaded to try and put my answer on paper— and if when I have finished, there are a few points cleared up that you have been wondering, and perhaps worrying about, I shall feel repaid for the writing. They say that "the pen is mightier than the sword," but my experiences of the last ten years have given me much more practice with the latter than with the former. I shall not attempt a flowery story, nor exaggerate anything to make it sound big, but I shall, as they say in the Court, tell "the truth, and nothing but the truth."

My story begins when this war broke out in August, 1914. I was working with a survey party at the time not far from Fernie, British. Columbia. I remember the day that I made up my mind to enlist. I had just decided the question when along came my chum Stevens, and I said, "Well, I'm jumping the job this morning, Steve." He said, "Why? What the devil is eating you now? Don't you know when you are well off?" I said, "Yes, Steve, I do; but it is like this—ever since you and I went to town the other day I have been thinking this thing over." "Thinking what?" "Why, about the war, of course—I can't get it out of my head. There is going to be the devil of a scrap over there—and say, boy! I've got to get into it! When I hear of what Germany is doing to poor little Belgium it makes my blood boil—I have worked with the Germans, and I have a little idea of what it would mean to turn the world over to them—so I'm off to draw my time." Well, when I came back from the boss's cabin, I found Steve packing up, and I said, "Why, what's the matter, Steve?" He said, "Oh hell! if you're going, I'm going too;" so we started off together.

We had a twelve-mile hike to the nearest town, and that night we took the train for Winnipeg. We stayed off in Moose Jaw to see some boys that we knew, and of course we told them that we were on our way to enlist. To our surprise we found that they were planning to join a company that was being recruited in Moose Jaw, and they urged us to sign up with them. We thought it would be nice to be with some one we knew, so one morning we lined up with three or four hundred others to be examined for the Army. They had room for only two hundred and fifty men, and as we stood in line we looked around to size up the bunch and see what our chances were for getting in. They were a husky-looking lot, and all were eager to go. I remember one big fellow near the end of the line offered me five dollars for my place. I said, "Go to hell with your five dollars." Afterwards in the trenches, when we were knee-deep in mud and the big shells were bursting around us, he could have had my place and welcome. Well, we were all taken on, and we got our first taste of drilling and marching. For about a week we were marched around the streets of Moose Jaw—flags were flying—bands playing—and we were the centre of interest. The last night we were there, the city tendered us a banquet and an old South African veteran gave us a farewell speech. Among other things, he said, "Well, boys, you belong to the Army now [they didn't let us forget it very long]. The first

Jack O'Brien

thing you must learn is discipline," and he gave us a long speech on that. Then he went on: "The next thing is cleanliness. I suppose you have been taught as I was that 'cleanliness is next to godliness'; but in the Army you will find that it works pretty much the other way—godliness is next to cleanliness." This is all I remember of the old soldier's speech, and afterwards, believe me, I found that he was right; in the trenches cleanliness is quite as difficult as godliness.

Well, early next morning we took the train for Winnipeg, and there was a big crowd to see us off, for most of the boys who had joined up had their homes in Moose Jaw. I didn't know any one, and I was not paying much attention to the crowd when a funny thing happened. I was feeling a bit lonely seeing all the other boys being made a fuss over, when suddenly a nice-looking young girl loomed up in front of me, and a joyful voice said, "Why, Harry, here you are; I have been looking all over for you." Now, my name was not Harry, but when she lifted her face to be kissed, why I tried to do as the real Harry would have done. Perhaps I did not succeed, for somehow she realized her mistake and she did not seem half as well pleased over it as I was. Finally the train pulled out amid the cheers of the crowd, and the boys who were leaving home and friends looked just a wee bit quiet and sad, but soon they recovered their spirits, and we had a jolly time playing cards and getting acquainted. They were all strangers to me, and we were destined to go through experiences that drew us closer together than brothers, but I didn't know it then, so I sat there and tried to imagine what they were like, and the opinions I formed were far from right in the light of events that followed. I have learned now how foolish it is to judge a man by his appearance. It was only a twelve-hour trip to Winnipeg, and when we got there we found a band to meet us. We were marched through the streets, and though we stuck out our chests and tried to remember all that had been told us about marching, I fear we made a poor impression. We still wore our ordinary clothes and only the badges on our arms marked us as would-be soldiers.

After about an hour's march we were taken to a large frame barrack known as the Horse Show Building. This place had been built for a skating rink and was never intended as a dwelling-place for men. In the winter the water poured from the frost-lined roof, and for a long time we had no floor. We slept on ticks filled with straw, and these were soaked every day—we were almost drowned out. There was an old piano in the building, and every morning we were awakened by a wag in the crowd playing "Pull for the shore, sailor." The boys would all take it up, and in a few minutes every one would be singing at the top of their voices. This put us in good humour for the day.

We were not the only ones in the building; other companies had come in from the West, and when our numbers had reached the 1,100 mark we were formed into what was known as the 28th Northwest Battalion.

Now, it is not my intention to give a detailed account of our training. We were like every other new battalion, perfectly green in the art of soldiering, awkward in the use of our hands and feet, but strong in our determination to make good as a battalion. Especially were we anxious to please our commanding officer. Just to give you an idea of how green I was, let me tell you of my first meeting with our O. C., Colonel Embury. I was lounging around the guardroom one day when the Sergeant asked me to take some papers to the Orderly Sergeant upstairs. Now, my tunic was unfastened, my belt loose, and my cap on the back of my head, but it never occurred to me to fix myself before going up. I took the papers and went up three steps at a time. When I reached

Jack O'Brien

the orderly-room I walked in, and said, "Who is the Orderly Sergeant here?" A voice from the corner of the room said, "Here, lad," and I started in his direction when another voice spoke up and said, "Look here, sonny—" I turned around and found myself looking into the genial fatherly face of Colonel Embury. I was too much surprised and dismayed to even attempt a salute, and the Colonel, instead of calling me down, just smiled and said: "Young man, supposing you go out into the hall, fasten up your tunic, tighten your belt, and put your cap on properly; then come to the door and knock. When you get an answer, walk in and salute, and see how much smarter and better it will look." You bet I felt cheap, and almost any sized hole would have been large enough for me just then. But I went out and did as I was told, and when I came back he answered my salute and smilingly said, "Now, that is fine," and went on with his work. What wouldn't a boy do for an officer who used him like that?

It was hard for us boys who had been on our own hook for several years to get used to the discipline of the Army. We were used to doing exactly as we liked, and the unquestioning obedience demanded did not come easy. Gee, but it used to hurt to take a "call-down" from a petty officer without having a chance to reply or even to show what we felt in our faces, and when he had said everything he could think of we had to touch our cap and say "Yes, Sir!" I assure you, very often we felt like saying something entirely different.

Training in the open with the thermometer ranging anywhere between 25 and 40 below zero is no fun. We were taught to shoot, march, skirmish and drill, and we also learned the art of "old soldiering," which means the art of being able to dodge anything in the shape of work. By the way, they have a fancy name for work in the Army—they call it "Fatigue," but when you come to do it it's just the same as the common variety spelled with four letters. We did not get meals at barracks, but took them in a restaurant downtown—and rising at 6 A.M. on a bitterly cold winter's morning and having to walk a mile to breakfast was not always pleasant. Sometimes we would break away and take a streetcar, till an order was issued forbidding our doing it. However, one very cold morning following a heavy fall of snow we plodded our way downtown; our new uniforms with their unlined greatcoats (minus the cozy fur collars such as civilians wore) did not keep out more than a quarter of the cold, the rest went through us. Our caps were wedge-shaped affairs of imitation black fur, and on mild days we felt very smart in them, but when it was forty below and Jack Frost was on a still hunt for every exposed portion of our body, a cap that would not be coaxed down to meet our collars was a fit object for our worst language.

Well, on this particular morning every one got half frozen going down, and after breakfast no one felt like walking home. About half of the boys "fell out" and took the street-car. I got on a car that was pretty well filled with our lads, and we were having a jolly time when the car stopped and in walked our O. C. Several of the boys jumped up to offer their seat, but the Colonel smiled and said, "Never mind, boys," and continued to stand at the back of the car. We were pretty quiet, for we hated to be caught disobeying orders, and especially did we hate being found out by our O. C. Well, he got off the car before we did, and we did not see him again till the next parade. Then when we were lined up Colonel Embury read out the rule forbidding us to break ranks—we were wondering how many days C. B. we would get—when the O. C. looked around with a smile and said, "Well, boys, I'll let you off this time, I didn't feel much like walking myself." One of the boys dug me in the ribs and whispered, "Some scout, eh?" It was little things like this that won the hearts of "his boys," as he always called us, and so far from spoiling discipline it made us put up with any discomforts for the sake of pleasing him.

But before going any farther I wish to explain what C. B. means. It is the favourite mode of punishment in the Army and is served out for almost all offences or "crimes," as they are called—the only variation being in the length of time given. "C. B." is "confined to barracks" and having to answer a bugle call every half-hour, after the battalion is dismissed. The object of answering this bugle call is to let the powers that be know that you are still there. In the Army it is known as "Defaulters," but we named it the "Angel Call." There was usually one or more of our little circle answering it, and the favourite crimes were smoking on parade, staying out without a pass, coming home "oiled," and staying in bed after reveille in the morning; the last-named was a favourite one of mine, and I escaped punishment for quite a while, but the old saying "The pitcher that goes oft to the well is sure to get broken at last" was true in my case. I had formed the habit of lying in bed and reading the paper for about half an hour after reveille, and it always made the Sergeant mad. However, so far he had not reported me; but this morning, after about twenty-five minutes of stolen comfort, the Sergeant said, "Now, look here, O'Brien, if you are not out of bed in three minutes I'll have you up before the Major." I looked, listened, and pulling out my watch continued reading. Exactly on the three minutes I jumped out, but the boys were all laughing and the Sergeant got mad and had me "pinched"; so at 9 a.m. I was brought up on the "carpet" before the Major. I was looking the picture of innocence, and I had a chum outside to prove that I was out of bed three minutes after the Sergeant's warning. Well, the Sergeant didn't press the charge very much, and the Major asked me how long it was after reveille when I got up. I said it was five minutes anyway, and I had them arguing whether it was five or ten minutes (it was really half an hour), when the officer said, "O'Brien, have you any witnesses?" I said, "Yes, Sir, Private Gammon." Officer: "Private Gammon, step forward. How long after reveille did O'Brien lie in bed?" "Fifteen minutes, Sir," said Gammon, and looked at me as though he were doing me a great favour. "Five days C. B.," said the Major; "right about turn, dismiss." Now, believe me, what I said to that boy wouldn't look well in print. No more "witnesses" for me—like the darky who was brought up before the judge for stealing chickens. He protested his innocence, and the judge said, "Pete, have you any witnesses?" The old man answered, "No, Sir, I never steals chickens 'fore witnesses." In the future I would follow my old schoolmaster's advice; he said, "My boy, never tell a lie; but if you do happen to tell one, make it a good one and stick to it." I haven't always been able to live up to the first part, but when I fell down on that the latter half came in handy. This was my first crime, but it wasn't by any means my last. I remember one day in the early spring the battalion was out doing some skirmishing, and somehow three of us got separated from the others. In looking for our company we came across an inviting-looking spot, and we sat down to have a rest. Smoking and telling stories made the time pass quickly, and when we came to look for the battalion it had gone home. We hiked for home as fast as our legs could carry us and got in about an hour late. Next morning we were paraded before the Major, and he listened to our story but evidently didn't sympathize with our love for nature and gave us seven days C. B. I thought the punishment rather stiff, but the old Major had it in for me. A few days before, when we were on parade, the old Major kept our platoon drilling after the others had gone in, and all the boys were sore. He gave us an order, and one of the boys near me said in a loud undertone, "Go to hell, you spindle-legged old crow." The Major heard it; he turned quickly and looked in our direction and caught me laughing, so he felt pretty sure that it was I who had made the remark; so when he got a chance to get even, he soaked it to me.

However, two can play at that game, and my chance came a few nights later; I was on sentry duty and the old Major was acting as orderly officer. He was always spying on us boys, and about 2 A.M. on the coldest nights he would make the round of the guards to be sure that we were all at our posts. This was not done by the other officers, and naturally we resented it, so when the boy on the next beat gave me the tip that the old boy was coming I stood in close to the wall and waited—as he turned the corner, stealing along like a cat, I sprang out with my bayonet at his chest, and in a voice loud enough to be heard ten blocks away shouted "Halt!" Old "Spindle-legs" threw up his hands, gasped like a fish, and it seemed half a minute before he whispered "Orderly officer." Of course I lowered my rifle with a fine show of respect, but he didn't lose any time asking what my orders were for the night; he beat it for the orderly-room as fast as his trembling legs could carry him. He took it for granted that we were *very much* on guard. The other guard and I almost had a fit laughing, and it was as much as we could do to face him next day.

Little things like this relieved the monotony of the days that otherwise were very much alike. We were drilled into shape and finally we came to take pleasure in doing things in the sharp brisk manner they required and in making as good a showing as possible—everything was for the honour of the battalion, and woe betide any one who was slovenly in his dress or who bungled his marching.

But we would have had a pretty lonely winter if it had not been for the great kindness shown us by some of the Winnipeg churches and also by individual ladies. Chief among these, I would like to take the liberty of mentioning Lady Nanton; she was the guardian angel of the 28th; the billiard room of her beautiful home was thrown open for our use every night in the week and a lunch was served to as many boys as cared to go. It was through the efforts of Lady Nanton that a smoking-room was erected for our benefit, for we were not allowed to smoke in barracks. I received parcels from her when I was a prisoner of war in Germany, and I leave you to imagine how much they were appreciated then; and now that the 28th boys are coming back wounded and broken in health it is Lady Nanton that still acts as guardian angel and gets everything possible for them.

But to go back to my story. We had been in training for about six months and the Army life had done a great deal for us. The city was full of soldiers; new battalions were being formed all the time, and we felt quite like old veterans. We were "fed up" with marching around the city on parade, and we longed to get into the real fighting. For my part, I was heartily sick of the whole thing, and all that made it bearable was the close friendship I had formed with some of the boys in my platoon; about a dozen of them were my close friends. I shall name a few of these, so that you may recognize them when they appear farther on in my story; there were "Bink," Steve, Mac, Bob, Tom, Jack, Scottie, and also our "dear old Chappie"; the last-named was one of those quiet-going Englishmen who always mean what they say and who invariably addressed every one as "my deah chappie," but he was a good old scout and everybody liked him. Our Sergeant, known among the boys as "Yap," is another inte-resting character; his heart was the biggest thing about him and his voice came next. If he wanted you to do anything he spoke loud enough to be heard a mile away; if you didn't do as he ordered, you could never bring in the excuse of not having heard. Then there was our Corporal, who got the name of "Barbed-wire Pete," so called because when the order came to grow moustaches his attempt looked like a barbed-wire entanglement. Now for our Lance Corporal, who when he got to France was known as "Flare-pistol Bill." He early developed a mania for shooting up flares in the front-line trench at night. We had two Yankees in our bunch—"Uncle Sam," who was the oldest man in the platoon, and "Baldy," who only wore a fringe of hair. One day in the trenches one of the boys noticed Baldy scratching his head on a spot where there was still a little hair, and he said, "Hey, Baldy, chase him out into the open; you'll have a better chance to catch him there." Now, I realize that this bunch of boys may sound very commonplace to the average reader, but we went through more than one hell together and I found them white clear through, and heroes every one of them. They included farmers, firemen, business men, university men, hoboes, and socialists. Some mixture!—but it was out of this kind of stuff that our Canadian Army was made, and I am not ashamed of their record.

Now that I have introduced you to some of my friends, I will go back to the time when we left Winnipeg. After many false rumours, at last the day came when we were to start. On the 26th of May, 1915, the order came out that we were to entrain the following morning—we were all confined to barracks and every one was crazy with joy—we hurried through our packing, then we sat around all night, singing, telling yarns, and trying to put in the time till morning. Early next day we were marched to the station, and though for obvious reasons our going had not been advertised, hundreds of friends were there to see us off. They loaded us with candy, fruit, smokes, and magazines, and I don't think a happier bunch ever left Winnipeg. The train trip was very uneventful. We ate and played cards most of the day. This was varied by an occasional route march around some town on the way. When we reached Montreal we were reviewed by the Duke of Connaught, and as soon as this was over they marched us down to our boat. After locating our berths we thought we had nothing to do but go out and do the city. My chum and I made our way down to the gangway and there found our way barred by a sentry who said, "Nobody allowed off the ship." We were terribly disappointed, but we had learned not "to reason why" in the Army, so we went to the other end of the ship. Here we found another boat drawn up alongside, and as there was no one in sight we boarded her. From here we had no trouble getting ashore, and away we went uptown—"stolen pleasure is the sweetest kind"—and we had no end of a time for a few hours. We hiked back and got to the ship just in time to turn in with the other boys; no one had missed us for a wonder, and everything was all right. Next morning we awoke to find ourselves slipping down the broad St. Lawrence. Our voyage lasted ten days, and it sure was "some" trip. The weather was perfect and we had all kinds of sport, wrestling, boxing, and everything that could be done in a limited space. The regimental band of the 28th was something that we were justly proud of, and they supplied the music for our concerts and dances—yes, we did have dances, even though there were no ladies present—half of the fellows tied handkerchiefs on their sleeves and took the ladies' part; their attempts at being ladylike and acting coy were very laughable. The only thing that really marred our pleasure was the lifeboat drill; any hour of the day or night when the signal was given, no matter what we were doing, we must grab our life-belt and make all possible speed to our place at the lifeboats. At first it was great fun, but soon we grew to hate it, and we almost wished the ship would be torpedoed just to make a change. The last three days of our trip we were in the "Danger Zone," and at night all lights were put out and as many men as possible slept on deck; machine guns were posted and men on duty at them all the time. The sentries had orders to shoot any one that showed a light. We were obliged to wear our life-belts night and day, and if I looked as funny to the others as they did to me, I don't see how they ever got their faces straight. Most of our waking hours were spent in looking for "subs," and every one that saw a bottle or stock on the water was sure he had sighted a periscope. One night as I was sleeping on deck I was awakened by having a great light flashed in my face—I jumped up in a hurry and to my amazement I found two great searchlights sweeping our ship from stern to stern— and immediately, out of the darkness, two destroyers, slim and grey, came racing up, one on either side of us. They gave us our first glimpse of Britain's sea power, and we felt a wonderful sense of security. In the morning we had a good look at the destroyers, for they were quite close and they kept just abreast of us—every now and then they would put on speed and rush ahead leaving us as if we were standing still—then they would turn almost in their own length and come rushing back, sometimes circling the ship two or three times. They reminded me of a couple of puppies gambolling and trying to coax the old dog into the game.

We proceeded this way till we hit the Channel, and soon we caught our first glimpse of the shores of England (or "Blighty," as the soldiers call it). The green hills sure did look good to us after gazing at water for ten days. We also passed a big wooden ship built in the time of Nelson that is being used as a training-ship for cadets—as we steamed slowly by, hundreds of the cadets were clustered on the masts and rigging, and they gave us a great burst of cheers. It was our first welcome to the old land. That night we slipped slowly into port, and again we caught a glimpse of Britain at war; big searchlights glaring out to sea, crossing and recrossing, searching—searching all the time. Big ships were going to and fro with coloured lights to show their identity. We stayed on the ship all night, but most of us were too excited to get any sleep. Next morning we were taken off and put aboard a dinky little train. The locomotives and coaches looked so small in comparison with the big American trans-continental trains that the Englishmen in our outfit came in for lots of chaff. "Baldy," the American, would say to Bob Goddard, "Do you call this miniature thing a railroad? Why, at home we have trains as big as this running up and down the floors of our restaurants carrying flapjacks." Of course every one roared at this, and Bob said, "Never mind, you can laugh now, but wait till we start and see the speed we have." They argued on this for a while, and then Bob said, "Why, the locomotives over here pick up water on the fly." "Aw, that's nothing," said Baldy; "they pick up hoboes on the fly in the States." Bob had nothing to say to this, and conversation lagged for a while. Some time later Bob called our attention to the really lovely scenery we were passing through. Said he, "Look at those lovely old trees with the creepers on them; where in the States would you find anything to compare with them?" But Baldy was ready, "Aw, I can see you were never in a lumber camp." "What difference does that make?" says Bob. "All the difference in the world," answered Baldy; "if you were ever in a lumber camp, you'd know without my telling you that we have men there with creepers on them." This was too much for Bob, and he quit;—we played cards the rest of the way to London, but when we reached it we became interested again in the outside world. London was a place we had all heard of, but few of us had seen. Bob was nearly crazy, for we passed in sight of his home. Of course he had been away for several years, but his people still lived there; it sure was hard for him to be so near and not be able to stop and see them. He showed us all the points of interest that were in sight; but our first impression of London was rather disappointing, for we were either going through suburbs or smoky tunnels. We went through some crowded districts, and the people all ran out and cheered us as we passed. England was going wild over Canadians then, for it was just after the Second Battle of Ypres, where our boys had made such a name for themselves. On one street there were about five hundred kids, and Baldy remarked, "No race suicide here."

Jack O'Brien

Pretty soon we left London and we all went back into the train. There was great speculation as to what camp we were bound for, but no one knew, and when at last the train came to a halt we were glad to get off and stretch our legs,—we stretched them a whole lot more than we intended before the night was out,—for we had to hike about four miles with full pack and then climb a long steep hill. We had nothing to eat all day and we were just like ravening wolves, but after we reached camp we had to wait for the cooks to prepare some "mulligan" (stewed beef) and tea; then we were lined up and bundled into our tents, about ten men in each. Next morning some of us were sent down to unload the transport and the rest were put to work setting things to rights at the camp. I was with those that went down to the depot, and here the battalion suffered its first casualty—the pet of the whole regiment was lying dead in the box-car—and though to an outsider he was only a bulldog, to us he was our beloved "Sandy," the mascot of our battalion. He had shared all our route marches, no matter what the weather, and as I saw him lying there I thought of the fun we used to have with him. Scores of times I have seen him, when the bugle sounded for us to fall in, go and take his little blanket from the low nail where it always hung, and beg one of the boys to put it on for him. He would wag himself almost to pieces trying to attract attention, and of course the boy wouldn't let on to notice him; so he would go from one to the other, till at last some one's good nature overcame the desire for further sport, and his blanket was fastened on. Then, with a glad bark, he would dash out and take his place at the head of the battalion. He knew the other bugle calls too, and the call to mess was answered by mad jumping and much showing of teeth. He responded with the officers to the Colonel's Parade, and as the officers formed a circle round Colonel Embury to receive their orders for the day, it was funny to see old Sandy right in the centre gazing up into the Colonel's face. Our O. C. loved him and always gave him his share of attention after the officers were dismissed—it was our Colonel who insisted on Sandy having his own bunk and blankets just like any of the men—so, after being such a pet, you can imagine how we felt when we saw him lying there dead, and we realized that we were to blame for his death. All dogs entering England have to spend several weeks in quarantine, and to save him from this some of the boys had boxed him up and placed him in the baggage car, but whoever had done the job was not careful to place him right side up, and when we opened the box poor old Sandy was lying on his back dead. The whole battalion mourned his loss, and our Colonel most of all. Well, after we got everything loaded up, we went back to camp, and there we found the boys as busy as bees—we were telling them about Sandy when suddenly we heard a humming sound—every one gazed skyward, and across the camp flew one of the British dirigibles. What a sight it was to us! The big cigar-shaped, silver-coloured airship dipped and climbed, and finally came down so low that we could plainly see the men in it. You should have heard the cheer we gave them. We watched it till it disappeared out across the sea. After awhile we got used to seeing airships of all kinds and we took no notice of them, but at first they were very interesting.

Another thing that happened on our first day in camp (by the way, we were quartered in Shorncliffe, right on the seacoast) —a few of us were standing looking across the Channel to France, and wondering what was happening there, when *boom-boom-boom*! we heard the guns in Belgium. We could hardly believe our ears. I don't know about the other fellows, but it sent a queer feeling through me to know that only fifty or sixty miles away our boys were fighting and dying. Before this the war had seemed very unreal, but the sound of the guns made me realize that it was a grim reality, and I wondered how I would face it when the time came.

Jack O'Brien

Well, the next few days saw us settled in camp and then our training commenced in real earnest. We thought the six months' training in Canada had made us hard, but what we went through for the next two months made us like nails. We had shooting, skirmishing, night marches, trench-digging, besides all the special courses. Three other battalions were in the same camp—the 27th from Winnipeg, 31st from Calgary, and the 29th from Vancouver—and the four of us were formed into what was called the "Sixth Brigade"; after the Battle of St. Eloi they were known as the "Iron Sixth." The only thing we objected to in the training was the length of time it took. It seemed as hard to get to France as it had been to get to England. We didn't eat from tables as we had in Canada, but each of us was provided with exactly the same equipment as they have in France,—namely, a mess tin. When the meal was called we would all line up, and meat and potatoes and everything would be dished into our can; then we would hike off to our tents and eat it sitting on the ground. Each day an orderly officer went the rounds to ask if there were any complaints, the usual procedure being to stick his head in the tent flap and say, "Any complaints, boys?" and walk on without waiting for an answer. One day he came to our tent and standing in the tent door asked the usual question. One of the boys was a college-bred Englishman, and he spoke up and said, "Oh, I say, old chap, there's no complaint, but, deah boy, I wish you would take your foot out of my mess tin—you are spoiling all my dinnah." The officer and the boys just roared. I suppose most of us compared it with the picturesque language we would have made use of.

Bob went home on leave about this time, and while in London he ran across an old schoolmate of his who was also home on leave. The lad's name was Harold Rust. He had spent several years in Canada, but happened to be in England when the war broke out and he had joined up with a London regiment. He had been one of Kitchener's "Contemptible Little Army" and had seen considerable service in France—he had been wounded and at the time Bob met him was home on sick leave—but he had been in America too long to enjoy the discipline of the British Army, and as he said himself he was "fed up" with it. So he asked Bob if there was any chance of getting into our brigade. He had tried several times to get a transfer into the Canadians, but each time he was turned down, so he said if Bob could get him in he would desert his own regiment and so save all the trouble of a transfer. Bob told him to send in an application to our Colonel, and shortly after Bob returned Colonel Embury sent for him. He said: "Goddard, I have here a letter from a man in London; he says he is a Canadian, and as all his chums are here, he wants to join the 28th. Do you know him?" "Yes, Sir, I knew him in Winnipeg," says Master Bob. "Well," said the Colonel, "we are one or two under strength, so I'll see what I can do." Bob came back tickled to death and told Tommy, Bink, and me all about it. If he got in we saw where we would have no end of fun having a fellow with us who had seen service in France and no one knowing it but ourselves. Well, a few nights later we were sitting in our tent foot-sore and dog-tired after an all-day route march when in walks Rust. Bob jumped up and made the introduction; he had been sent for to come down and take his medical examination. We wondered how he would ever get through without the Doctor seeing his wounds, but when he came up for his examination he got through by keeping his hand over the old scar. Next day he was attested, put into uniform, and then he was given leave to go home and fix up his business affairs. This is what he did—he changed on the train from khaki into civies, went home, put on his Imperial uniform, and went up to draw his regimental pay. He drew all that was coming to him, and tried to get an advance but failed. Then he went home, changed into his Canadian uniform, and leaving his other in a bundle, he came away without even letting his father know where he was going. He came down to Shorncliffe and we got him into our platoon and into our tent, and then the fun started. The boys thought him a greenhorn, and they were all showing him how to do things. He would let them help to put his puttees on, show him the hundred and one things that a soldier needs to know; we would almost burst trying to keep from laughing. When we were out drilling, he was just as clumsy as though he had never held a rifle—after him meeting the Germans in the open and firing till his rifle jammed. The Sergeant would take him out and give him private lessons, showing him how to slope arms and present arms, and all the time Rust was looking innocent and acting as awkward as the greenest of the green. Those of us who knew nearly killed ourselves laughing. Then they gave him another leave, and we didn't see any more of him till we were ready to leave for France.

Leave to London was very hard to get, and of course we were all crazy to go there; but we were all allowed late leave on Sundays, and of course we always had our Saturday afternoons, so if we could dodge the military police we took the train at noon on Saturday and spent Sunday in London. There was an early morning train which got us in before reveille on Monday. We worked this successfully several times, but one Sunday almost our whole platoon was in London, and as luck would have it we all missed the early tram. When our platoon lined up there were only ten present, and of course this gave the whole thing away. We arrived on the noon train and we sure did get a calling down—of course we were forbidden to do it again. However, before going to France each of us had a week in London, and that wonderful old city was surely an eye-opener to us Western boys. In fact, England itself is like a big garden; and so beautiful that it's little wonder that its people would fight to the last man to save it. We had only been in England a short time when they started giving instruction in special courses, such as bombing, signalling, and machine gun work. Any one who took one of these courses was exempt from all fatigue duty, and they did not report so early in the morning. Steve and I joined the bombers, known in France as the "Suicide Club," and Bob, with two or three others, took up the machine gun work. I found the bomb throwing very interesting, and in our six weeks' course we learned to handle the "Mills" bomb, "hair-brush," and the "jam tin." There was just enough danger in it to make it exciting and there was some sport as well. For instance, the "jam tin" bomb is a real jam tin packed with explosive, and we had to make as well as throw them, and for practice we were allowed to bomb the trenches dug by our battalion. They would spend two or three weeks digging and fixing up a nice trench and then along would come the bombers and blow it all to smithereens—no wonder the boys were sore at us; but then, they were getting practice, and we were only doing what "Fritzie" would do for them later on. Steve and I stuck with the bombers, but one morning as I watched our battalion line up I was surprised to see Bob and his pals in the ranks. When we met that night I asked him why he had given up the machine gun work, and I sure did laugh at what he told me. He said: "Aw, I liked the work well enough, and it was fun to see how mad our Sergeant got when he came after us for picket or guard duties; we thought we had a snap sitting down listening to the machine gun officer's lectures, but what do you think he told us yesterday? Why, that in the event of a retirement machine guns were left behind to cover the retreat, and were sacrificed to save the main body of the Army! Now, wouldn't that be a devil of a fix to be in? No sacrifice stuff for mine—I don't mind taking my chance with the other boys, but I won't stay out there alone." Poor old Bob, we all roasted him about it, but he never went back. Shortly before leaving England almost the entire 10th platoon got leave, and we all went up to London, and I assure you the time we had wasn't slow. Bob and a few of the others whose homes were in

London spent part of the time there, but we had a whole week and we spent the last few days together. Among other places of interest, we visited Madame Tussaud's Waxworks, and it was here that Scottie slipped one over Bink. We were all standing at the entrance and Scottie said, "Bink, go and ask the attendant for a program." Bink walked up to the lady at the table, and in his most polite tone said, "Can you let me have a program?" Evidently the attendant didn't hear, for there was no answer, so Bink said in a louder tone, "Say, look here, I want a program"; still there was no response and Bink was beginning to look sore when Scottie yells out, "Come away from there, you darn fool; are you going to talk to that wax figure all day?" Scottie would have "cashed in" right there if Bink could have caught him.

The same day we had a good joke on Steve—he had heard that Leicester Lounge was a favourite meeting-place for Canadians, and he decided to go there and see if he could find any of the boys, so he hailed a taxi and gave the man orders to drive him to Leicester Lounge. The driver took him round a couple of blocks and then said, "Here's the place, Sir." Steve paid him and then looked around to find himself in the very spot he started from—he had been standing in front of Leicester Lounge when he took the taxi, and it is just as well that he does not know what that driver thought of him—however, he was sport enough to tell the joke on himself. Well, the week slipped by and we took a couple of extra days on our own account—of course we expected to pay up for it, but we thought it was worth it. Our next leave would be from France, and anything might happen before then. Well, we got back, and to our joy, we found that the Orderly Sergeant had got "soused" and forgot to mark us absent, so maybe we were not glad that we had those two extra days—the only crimes you are sorry for in the Army are the ones that are found out. Several times after this we took "French leave" and went up to London, and then we had our work cut out dodging the military police. Sometimes we were caught and then we had to pass a day or two in "Clink"—or, in other words, guard-room. We had bathing parade once or twice a week, and we would all go down and have a swim in the sea. Oh, it was great sport, and we were surprised to find it so easy to swim in the salt water. The country around our camp was very hilly and most of our route marches were made with full kit, so a long route march was anything but fun. Our two Americans took a delight in guying Bob about his love for scenery—poor old Bob would be sweating along under his heavy pack and one of the boys would call out, "Well, Bob, how do you like your scenery now?" Bob was silent, perhaps because he needed all his breath for walking, like the small steamboat that put on such a big whistle that it hadn't power enough to navigate and blow its whistle at the same time. But we did enjoy being sent on ahead as scouts to find out the lay of the country. We would travel till we came across some out-of-the-way "pub" or village inn, and there we would stay till it was time to go back to camp; then we would rejoin the battalion and give a lot of information that we had made up between us.

CHAPTER II

There was one big event that we will remember for the rest of our lives, and that was our review by the King and Lord Kitchener. We were reviewed on Sir John Moore's Plain, and the entire Second Division of Infantry as well as the Artillery was out that day; all the roads leading to the Plain were packed with troops, and as we all marched down and lined up in review order, it was the biggest bunch of soldiers I have ever seen together. There were somewhere between fifteen and sixteen thousand men, and when they were marching with fixed bayonets it looked like a sea of steel.

After lining up we had a long wait, and all at once a thunderstorm came up. The rain came down in pailfuls, and soon all the boys were singing "Throw out the life line, some one is sinking today." One of the boys near me said, "I don't see why the devil no one has ever thought of putting a roof over this blamed island." Well, just when we were in the middle of our song and the whole fifteen thousand men were roaring it out at the top of their voices, the King's automobile went by. We were soon put into marching order and the march past the King and Lord Kitchener commenced. When we got the order "Eyes right!" we looked at them both—the King was a smaller man than we expected to see, and Kitchener looked older than we thought he would be. But oh, what eyes Kitchener had! they seemed to be looking every man straight in the face—the boys all noticed the same thing, and spoke of it afterwards. After the march past the officers were called up and congratulated on the showing the men had made, and they passed it on to us. Well, away we went back to camp, wet and tired, but delighted over the events of the day and we all felt proud of being "Britishers." When we got back to camp and were talking things over, we all agreed that our inspection was a sign of an early departure for France, and from that on the place buzzed with rumours of when we were to start. It does not take much to start a rumour going in the Army—for instance, the Colonel buys a light shirt, and his batman tells somebody that he thinks we are going to a warm climate, as the Colonel is buying light clothes. The person he told it to passes it on this way—"Oh yes, the Colonel's servant says we are going to India," and No. 3 announces "I have it from some one high up that we are being sent to India instead of to France, the Colonel is laying in a supply of light clothes; and in the Quartermaster's store they have gotten in a supply of sun helmets"—and so it goes, increasing in size like the report of a German victory in their newspapers. But we soon saw that our stay was going to be short, for presently our new equipment was issued to us. This consisted of two khaki shirts, two heavy suits of underwear, two heavy army blankets, rifle and ammunition, hat covers, several pairs of socks, a lot of small things, and last but not least, two pairs of boots. Besides this, we had our haversack containing emergency rations: tea, sugar, army biscuits, and bully-beef. I put my pack on the scales when I got it all together, and it weighed just one hundred pounds.

Our new issue of boots came in for more attention than anything else. I must tell you about them; they were destined to cause us no end of misery in the near future. Such boots! "Gravel crushers," we called them. Big heavy marching boots, armour-plated on the sole and so large that they looked and felt like barges. In my childhood days I never could understand how the "Old Lady lived in a shoe," but when I saw these boots the mystery was solved; though, mind you, they were just the thing for France; and after they got broken in, we couldn't have had anything better. But after our light-weight boot manufactured out of paper by some of our patriotic(?) Canadian firms, it took some time to get our feet used to the heavier weight.

Just before we were ready to leave for France we were treated to an air-raid. Some Zeppelins came over and dropped bombs not far from our camp. Of course the warning was sounded, all lights put out, and we sat there as still as mice, wondering what was going to happen next. I fancy we felt something as a rabbit does when there is a keen-eyed hawk soaring overhead. However, the danger passed and there was no harm done, but they were evidently looking for our camp, for two days after we left it, it was properly bombed.

Well, after we got our equipment, we were kept busy for a couple of days signing sheets and undergoing kit inspection, but finally everything was attended to and we were ready to start. It was a hot day when we "fell in" for our eight-mile hike to—, and when I had all my kit in place, I think I must have looked like a snail who carries his house packed on his back. Well, the farther we went the heavier our load became. Our feet were tortured by the new stiff boots; some of the boys took theirs off and walked in their socks, but these had their feet cut and bruised by the stones which plentifully bestrewed our way. Oh, how we cursed our officers for making us wear our new boots for the first time on such a hike. We should have had them long enough ahead to get them broken in. Well, some of the boys fell out, but the rest of us struggled on, and at last, just at dark, we reached the pier. We were dripping with perspiration, and we had eaten nothing except our army ration. Well, we sat around till we all got cold; and then, to our utter amazement and disgust, the order came, not to embark, but to "right-about-turn"; and with much swearing and grousing, we commenced what was afterwards known among the 6th Brigade as "The Retreat from Folkestone." Of course the officers weren't to blame—some mines had broken loose in the Channel, and until they were looked after by the mine sweepers it wasn't safe to cross. Oh, that march! no one who went through it will ever forget what we went through. In all my experience in France, I never carried such a pack. And after going a short distance on the return trip, the boys, like sinking ships, began to get rid of their cargo—for miles that road was strewn with boots, shirts, sweaters, cap covers, all kinds of articles—then the boys themselves began to fall out, and the dog-tired men rolled themselves in their blankets and lay down in their tracks. By the way, we were not going back to Folkestone, but were bound for a place known as "Sir John Moore's Plain"; but nobody knew how far it was, nor the quickest way to get there; some went one way and some another. Our battalion kept on going with frequent rests; we were dripping with sweat, and when the men sat down to rest they were too tired and disgusted to even swear. Finally our officers turned to us and said, "Only another mile, boys," and our hopes revived a little; but meeting a civilian, I asked him how far it was to Moore's Plain, and he said, "Oh, it's about four miles." Our officer overheard and said "Come on, boys, let's make camp here," and No. 10 platoon quit right there. We were going through a little village at the time, and we piled up on the lawns, rolled out our blankets and went to sleep. Next morning the lady of the house who owned the lawn found us there; she took pity on us, and calling us in gave us our breakfast. Later, we were sitting on the lawn when our Colonel drove up in his automobile. He called, "Come on, boys, hurry up and get up to the camp." He told us how to go and then went on to round up the rest—so we drifted on towards the camp and finally reached it, and all that day the

Jack O'Brien

boys came straggling in, some of them still carrying their boots. Well, that night we had to pack up and march down again, but this time it wasn't so hot, and all our spare equipment went by transport. We reached the port about dusk and we were soon loaded up; as soon as we got on board, life-belts had to be put on, and the boat started immediately. We watched the lights of "Old Blighty" flicker and fade away; and every now and then we caught glimpses of destroyers as they went by and disappeared into the darkness. Finally the last lighthouse was passed—no more lights were to be seen, and I turned and looked towards France, wondering what was in store for me there. Little did I think that I would spend a year in Germany before I would see the English shores again.

It wasn't long before the lights of France came in sight. We watched them get clearer and clearer, and soon the command came to put our packs on. We were all ready to march by the time the boat was docked, and off we went. We were on the soil of France, and we all looked around curiously. The first thing I noticed was a French soldier on guard, and I saw that he presented arms in a different way to what we were used to, and also that his bayonet was about twice as long as ours. We soon passed him, and I don't remember much about the march that followed. We were dead-tired, and after travelling for what seemed hours over cobblestones we came to a steep hill—the boys commenced to swear, but we stuck to it for a while. Finally I gave up and lay down beside the road; by this time a lot of the boys had dropped out. After resting a while I started on again, and found Bink and Bob unrolling their blankets—I wanted them to come with me, but a sleep looked good to them. Tommy, Steve, and Baldy were doing the same thing, but instead of following suit I struggled on; at the top of the hill I found a bunch of tents, but that was all—the visions I had of a hot meal faded away, there was no grub in sight—I rolled into one of the tents, spread out my blankets, and had just closed my eyes, when a voice said, "O'Brien, you are on fatigue." I started to kick, but it was no use, so I followed the Sergeant out to where he had a bunch lined up; we were ordered to go down to the commissary tent about five hundred yards distant and draw rations. Well, away we went, and we spent the rest of the night carrying up boxes of jam, butter, bully-beef, and sardines. When I was carrying up the last two boxes, just at daylight, along came the other boys; they thought it was a great joke for them to be comfortably sleeping while I worked getting up grub for them to eat. I couldn't see the fun in it just then, and I told them so, but they only laughed the more. Well, I curled up in my blankets, and it seemed that I had just got to sleep when Tommy wakened me; breakfast was being served, and he had drawn mine. After my bacon and tea and a good wash I felt better.

While we were at breakfast a lot of little French kids crowded around, and we were all amused at the little beggars. Their speech, half French and half English, was very funny. But say, you should have seen them smoke! Little kids hardly able to walk were smoking just like old men. They seemed very hungry, and we gave them lots of our food until we found they were putting it into a sack to carry away.

Well, we stayed in camp till noon, and just after dinner we were told to get ready to move off. Soon we were marching down to take the train, and if the French people who watched us so curiously had seen us go up the night before they would not have recognized us as the same bunch. The French gave us a great reception; the girls brought us fruit, candy, and smokes, and our journey to the station was quite a triumphal procession. One of the girls came running up and gave me a couple of bottles—Rust was beside me and had been through it all before, so he whispered, "Put them in your pack; it is red wine." I guess I was a little slow in getting them out of sight, for our officer saw them and he said, "Don't touch that, it may be poisoned." Of course we had to be careful of spies, but I stuck the bottles in my pack when the officer wasn't looking. Well, we marched to the depot and were soon packed into the small uncomfortable coaches. We started to kick and grumble, but Rust said: "You are lucky to have coaches at all. Last time I went up I rode in a cattle-car," and he pointed out a lot of cars on which was painted "Capacity, so many horses, so many men." After that we hadn't anything more to say.

After much talking and jabbering by the French interpreters we finally got started, and we soon left L—h far behind. I got out my poisoned (?) wine, and not wanting to take any risks myself I politely let Baldy have the first drink. I waited a few minutes and he still looked well, so we finished it up. This put us in good spirits for the trip and every one was gay; no one would ever have imagined that we were on our way to the trenches. We were very much interested in the country we were passing through, but what struck us most forcibly was the number of soldiers we saw. Everywhere we looked there were crowds of them; we thought there were a lot in Blighty, but there seemed to be nothing else here. We passed big railway guns, and once a big Red Cross train glided slowly by—this made us think a bit—but we tried not to look into the future, for we realized that the horrible side of the war would come to us soon enough. Every time the train stopped the French kids would crowd around the coaches crying "Bully-beef, biscuits, cigarettes for my papa, prisoner in Germany." It was all new to us, and we gave them all we could spare. Later on we got wise to the kids, and we found that if we were soft-hearted or soft-headed, they would say the whole family were prisoners. One thing that surprised and shocked us was to hear the little kids swearing; they would use the most frightful oaths, and the funny part of it was that they gave them the pure cockney twang; I suppose they had heard and were imitating the Imperial troops. Well, after travelling all day we finally arrived in C— and we were marched off to our first billets. I belonged to "C" Company and we were quartered in a barn connected with a farmhouse. It was late when we arrived, and after we had supper we lay down in the straw and soon were all asleep; but it wasn't long before we became uneasy, and soon we were awakened by the feeling that some one or something was trying to bore holes in us. We twisted and turned, but the first ones to waken, tried to keep quiet, and it was not till every one was on the move that we realized that we had made our first acquaintance with the worst pest in the Army—body lice, or "cooties" as they call them—the straw on which we were lying was fairly alive with the little beasts. We thought it strange then, but nearly every billet where there is straw is the same; "soldiers come and soldiers go, but the same straw goes on forever." The next day we were busy boiling our shirts, but if we had only known we might have saved ourselves the trouble, for we were never free from the pests after that. All the belts and powders people send out only seem to fatten them—by the way, gas doesn't kill them either; I think they must have gas helmets. The day was spent in inspection, and the paymaster came and gave us our first pay in France, fifty francs; that night we were allowed downtown, and we made our first acquaintance with the French estaminets or wine-shops; they are only allowed to sell light wines, red and white, to the troops, and French beer. Well, one might just as well drink water. Rust had been through the mill before and could speak French pretty well, and was soon jabbering to the old Frenchwoman, whose face became all smiles when she found he had been wounded at Ypres; her husband had also been wounded there. We wandered in and out every place in the village till it was time to go back to billets. The next day we had to smarten up and get ready for the Brigadier-General, who was going to inspect us. Brigadier-General Ketchen was his name, and instead of a formal inspection he rode up, dismounted, came into the orchard where we were all lined up and said, "Dismiss the men, Major." The Major did so and the Brigadier then spoke to us: "Gather round, boys, I want to have a little talk with you. You've been under my command about nine months now, and I've always been proud of you, and now you are going up the line, and I want to say this to you: Don't go up with any idea that you are going to be killed—we want you all to take care of yourselves and not expose yourselves recklessly—never mind if Bill bets Harry that he can stick his head over without being hit, for if he loses he can't pay. And remember a dead man is no use to us, we want you alive, and when we want you to put your heads up, we'll tell you! And I've no doubt that you will only be too eager. Now, your Colonel and myself have been in the trenches, where you are going, and you are relieving a regiment that has a name second to none out here; and I want you to have the same kind of a name. The food is fine—in fact, we were surprised to see so much and of such good quality in the front line. Above all, I want you to trust your officers as I trust them, and I'm sure they trust you. If at any time you think you are suffering any injustice, don't talk and grumble amongst yourselves, but let's hear about it, and if we can remedy it that's what we want to do. Now, I suppose this will be the last chance I have of talking to you before you go in the trenches, and I don't think there is much more to say. We have a long hike ahead of us tomorrow, and you will march through a town where corps headquarters are, and thousands of soldiers will be there, and I want you to show, by your marching and march discipline, that as soldiers and fighting men Canadians are second to none. That's all, boys!" We thought quite a lot of his speech and the simple way in which it was delivered, and we got to discussing things and sharpening our bayonets and doing a lot more fool things. The place where we were had been occupied by Germans early in the war, a Uhlan patrol having stayed there, and the Frenchman showed a Uhlan lance and scars on the doors and sides of the barn where fragments of shell had struck when they had been chased out. The next day we formed up bright and early, and away we marched. We had not gone far when every neck was craned up, watching some little black and white dots in the sky. I asked Rust what it was. "Oh, anti-aircraft guns shooting at an aeroplane," said he. We strained our eyes, but it was a long way off and high up, and we couldn't see the aeroplane. Later on we saw what looked like big sausages up in the sky. They were the big observation balloons, and so we kept on, something new and interesting all the time. We passed lots of troops out in their rest billets; muddy and dirty some of them looked; they watched us in amused contempt as we swung proudly by, as much as to say, "Wait till you've been through what we have, you won't look so smart." We soon came to B—, and with the regimental band at our head playing, "Pack all your troubles in your old kit-bag" we marched through in great shape. At sundown we reached camp, tired, all in, but still interested. We were quartered in huts close to an old ruined town, and we were within shell fire. Directly we had supper we were outside watching the shells burst about a mile away; I don't think we ever thought of Fritz shelling us. Aeroplanes were flying overhead and our guns were keeping up an incessant roar, but it seemed more on our right; afterwards we knew that it was the big bombardment before the Battle of Loos. We all slept well that night and were up early the next morning. We lounged around all day, and a party of officers and N.C.O.'s went to look over the trenches we were going in. Just at nightfall it started to rain, a cold wet drizzling rain, and when we fell in, it looked as if we were in for a wetting, and we were. We were carrying our packs, and as we started off we were all feeling fine, and if it hadn't been for the rain we wouldn't have minded. I often laugh when I think of that march; we were miles away from any Germans when we started, yet we spoke in whispers,—of course we didn't know any better then,—and whenever a flare went up we stopped, then went on again. We could see where the trenches were as flares were continually going up, lighting up things for a while and then dying out. At last we met some men from the battalion that we were going to relieve, and they acted as guides; past tumble-down houses, along roads full of holes, in and out of mudholes. We were very careful at first, but we might just as well have walked through the lot, for we were all mud to our knees when we got in. We at last entered the communicating trenches and we followed each other, cracking a joke now and again to keep our spirits up; every little while whiz! would go a bullet overhead and we ducked our nuts—we were perfectly safe if we had only known. We passed some Highlanders (Canadians); I suppose they must have been amused at us, as we were all eager to know where the Germans were—I think we had an idea that we were going into a bayonet charge every morning before breakfast. Soon we came to a place where the trench jogged in and out, and in every jog were men standing up and looking across into the blackness; we were in the front line. After much confusion we at last relieved the others. Listening-posts had to be placed and machine guns manned and lots of other things done. We soon found out that one could look over at night and be comparatively safe; there was always a certain amount of rifle fire, but one can't aim at night and the bullets mostly go high. At last day dawned, and we were quite surprised to find that nothing had happened; Scottie and I had our breakfast,—the cook cooked it, and it was distributed in the trench,—then we were put on sentry to watch through the periscope, while the rest had a sleep. We were sitting there talking things over when we heard a roaring noise overhead, and a bing-bang! in the town which lay behind our trenches. We thought it was aeroplanes dropping bombs, and Scottie and I looked for them but we couldn't see anything. At last an officer came along and we asked him.

"Oh yes," said he, "those are German shells." Well, after a few days in the trenches we went back to a place called L— for a rest, or rather we were in reserve. We were now in what was known as the Kemmel Shelters; here we turned night into day—we slept or did nothing in the daytime, but at night we worked like bees—we were busy on fatigue parties carrying up ammunition and provisions to the front lines. Now, don't run off with the idea that this is a bomb-proof job; Fritzie knows all about the supplies that must be brought up, and you can bet your sweet life that he takes a delight in picking off rationing parties, and such-like. Every night our supports were heavily shelled; every road leading to the lines had a battery trained on it and every little while it was swept by shrapnel. We gradually got used to the danger, and if they started to shell the road we were on we would flop into a ditch or shell hole till the storm had passed. Speaking of this reminds me of something that happened in that first week. A party of us were carrying coke to the front line, and we had two sacks each; I had mine tied together and hung around my neck (the way I wore my red mittens when I was a youngster). We walked single file, and the boy ahead called back, "Shell hole, keep to the right," but it was too late for me, one foot had gone in and the weight of the coke made me lose my balance, so in I plunged head first; there was four feet of water in that hole, to say nothing of the soft juicy mud at the bottom, and I gurgled and gasped and was almost drowned before I could free myself from the coke. Finally I struggled out, and without waiting to recover my cargo I made a bee-line for my billet—the boys were fairly killing themselves laughing, and I don't blame them *now*, for I must have been a pretty-looking bird; I was plastered from head to foot with mud, and dirty water streamed over my beautiful features. Well, after a week of this night duty we were sent eight miles back to "Rest Billets"—here we got a bath— which I assure you was very welcome—also some clean clothes, but we didn't succeed in shaking our friends the

Jack O'Brien

"cooties";—like the poor, they were always with us. While on rest we were quartered in some frame huts, and these extended for a quarter of a mile on either side of the road. Between the huts and the road there was an immense ditch, and this usually contained a couple of feet of muddy water; the boys had planks leading from their huts to the road. One night one of the boys came home loaded and he attempted to cross one of these planks—in the darkness he missed his footing and *flop*! he went into the water; he found himself sitting in about two feet of slushy mud and he put down his hands to push himself up, but the mud was sticky and he only succeeded in going in deeper. We heard him calling for help, and when we got to him only his head and toes were above water; the air around looked very blue, but I don't believe the Recording Angel put down everything he said. He looked so funny we could hardly help him for laughing.

Well, our week's rest was over all too soon for us, and we were sent back to the front lines. This was the routine that we followed that winter; one week in the trenches, one at the supports, and one on rest. We had been up to the trenches three times before we had our first brush with Fritzie; the Battle of Loos was being fought to the southward, but things had been comparatively quiet with us. However, one evening when we were "standing to," just at sunset, suddenly the ground that we were standing on began to rock—we pitched too and fro like drunken men—and farther down the trench the earth opened and a flame of fire shot up into the air. It looked more like a volcano in eruption than anything else, and we couldn't imagine what was happening. Someone yelled, "The Germans are coming!"; but our officer said, "Don't be frightened, boys; a mine has been exploded." The German artillery then opened up a terrific bombardment, and they were answered by our guns, and for about an hour it certainly seemed as if hell had been let loose. We were afraid to take shelter in our dugouts, for we thought that Fritzie might come over any moment, and sure enough, as soon as their gun fire slackened, we saw them coming. It was an exciting moment when we got our first sight of them, and I know I trembled from head to foot; but we opened fire on them and as soon as I began shooting, all fear left me—they never got farther than their own wire entanglements—the rapid fire from our rifles and the support of our guns was too much for them. No doubt they expected to find us all dead after the explosion and the shelling they had given us, but we showed them that we were still very much alive. We "stood to" all that night, but nothing further happened. Just at dawn I peeped over the parapet, and it looked as though some one had been hanging out a wash; their wire entanglements were full of German uniforms. Of course we were not allowed to leave our post during the night in case of another attack, but when morning came we looked around to see what damage the mine had done; we found that about fifty of our brave boys were either killed or wounded—this was the first break in our ranks, and it made us feel very sore—you could put a good-sized house in the crater made by the explosion, and it was to occupy this that the Germans had come over. The crater was immediately organized as a listening-post and ever afterwards it was known as the "Glory Hole." It was always the hottest part of our trench, and many a night I spent in it. The German trench was only thirty yards away, and they could lob bombs in on top of us. To improve matters, old "Glory" always contained at least two feet of water, and on a cold rainy night it was "some job" standing at listening-post, two hours at a stretch, up to the knees in water. When relieved, you had four hours off, and you would huddle up on the firing-step with your feet still in the water, and either smoke or try to get a little sleep. But, often it rained, snowed, and froze all in the same night, and I have had my clothes frozen so stiff that in the morning I could scarcely move.

But, to come back to our story. Next morning the killed and wounded were taken back of the lines, and things went on as before, only now we did not feel nearly so comfortable, knowing that at any moment the earth might open and up we would go. We were in the trenches one day when *shuz-z-z-shiz-bang*! the dirt flew, not far from us, but we couldn't see what had done it. Later we heard the same noise, and coming tumbling through the air was something that looked like a big black sausage; the moment it struck the ground it exploded with an awful concussion, and dirt and sandbags flew. It was a big trench mortar, and we soon found that if you saw it in time you could dodge it. Fritzie had a special spite at the "Glory Hole," and every little while he would strafe it. About this time we received our first supply of trench mortars, and I assure you we enjoyed using them. They were big round balls weighing about sixty pounds, and they looked something like the English plum pudding. We called them "Plum Puddin's." I don't know what Fritzie called them, but he got them whether he called them or not. They had long steel handles and were easily thrown; no doubt the Germans were just as busy dodging ours as we were getting out of the way of theirs.

For the next couple of months nothing of any importance happened, and all we seemed to do was fill sandbags with mud, dig new trenches, clean out old ones, and wade through mud; and such mud! so many men wading through it worked it up and made it like glue—in some places it was up to the waist and many a man got stuck and had to wait till some one came along and pulled him out—through it all our little bunch stuck together and had lots of fun laughing at each other's misfortunes. We were usually on the same working parties and listening-posts; working on the latter gave us eyes like cats, though I can tell you that it is no fun staring out into "No Man's Land" (the space between the German lines and ours) for hours at a time, not daring to move or speak. We had a wire with us connected with the trench, for a listening-post is always an advanced position, and we used a code of signals. One pull meant "Send up a flare, we want to have a good look around," two pulls "All's well," three "Hostile patrol is out in No Man's Land," and if we threw the bomb that we always carried it meant that the Germans were coming and it gave a general alarm. We had only had the one brush with Fritzie, and the discomforts of the trenches began to get on our nerves; we would much rather have been mixed up in the real fighting. Of course when we were off on rest we had clean clothes, better grub, and our letters and parcels from home; coming up to Christmas the latter became more numerous, and we usually found a bunch waiting for us. We were just like one big family, and the boys who got parcels shared up with those who hadn't any; Bob would pick up Tommy's parcel, look at the name, and say, "*We've* got a parcel."

Then came our first Christmas in the trenches, or rather in France. We were out at the support billets on Christmas Day, and after working all night we were much disgusted when our Sergeant came in where we were sleeping and told us we had to go up to the lines with some supplies. However, they gave us an issue of rum, and we started out. We had made our trip and were on the road back when a sniper caught sight of us. There was water in the communication trench, and my chum and I got out and walked on top; pretty soon a bullet passed between us but we did not pay any attention, we thought it must be an accident, but a few seconds later, another hit just ahead of us and we realized that we were the "centre of attraction," so we made a bound for the trench; just as we lit, another bullet struck just behind us, so we came pretty near getting a Christmas box from Fritz. We found that we had to take over the trenches that night, so there was not much fuss made over our Christmas dinner, but we had a little extra spread.

Jack O'Brien

However, when New Year's came we were at rest billet, and our beloved Colonel had planned a big dinner for us. It was served in an old schoolhouse and we had roast turkey, plum pudding, and almost everything you could mention, and the Colonel himself came in and carved the turkey for us. All that week on rest we had a glorious time, our parcels had arrived from home and every one was feeling happy.

Nothing of any importance happened in the next few weeks, things were pretty quiet on the line; of course it was raining most of the time and we were up to our knees in mud and water. We were four months without seeing the sun, and we were beginning to think that Fritzie had gotten his range and blown him out. Then too we were crawling with vermin, and even when we got a clean outfit of clothes in a few hours they would be just as bad as ever. Being wet all the time, and having to put up with the discomfort of vermin and rats, were harder on us than the dangers of actual fighting. The part of the line where we were had superior artillery positions and observation posts, and any time Fritzie opened up, our artillery soon silenced him. It used to be a case of "You let me alone, and I'll let you alone." The trenches were in awful shape in spite of the continuous working parties, each rain made them a little worse. We used to get our rum every morning, and I want to say a word to those at home who say it should be stopped. I would like to make them lie out in a wet mudhole all night, come in blue and cold and hardly able to stand, not knowing whether they had feet or lumps of ice attached to their legs, and see whether or not they would want something to warm them up—I think we would all have been dead if it hadn't been for the rum that winter. You see, you are "all in" after a night in the open, and all you want to do is to sleep, so you crawl into the nearest dugout and lie down; now, the rum just keeps the blood circulating and the body warm while you are sleeping, so that when you waken you have not caught the chill that otherwise yon would have done, for those dugouts of ours were anything but cozy and comfortable. They were really only little huts in the trench, each one large enough for two or three men. They were built up with sandbags and had a piece of corrugated iron over the top; for the floor there was usually two or three inches of wet mud. I assure you it was cold comfort, and we were not allowed to lie in peace even here—a rat would run over your face, or crawl over your body to see if there was anything eatable in your pockets. Every bit of eats about us had to be securely fastened up in our mess tins to save it from these pests. I remember one morning I came in from sentry duty, and after having breakfast I lay down in a dugout; we were given enough bread ration in the morning to last us all day, and what was over from my breakfast I put in my mess tin, but I had lost the cover of my tin, so I hung it up thinking it would be safe from the rats. Uncle Sam was sleeping when I came in, and I lay down beside him. I was enjoying a cigarette when all at once I saw a rat heading for my tin; I didn't want to get up to chase him away, so I reached over and brought up my rifle—there was scarcely room to use it in the dugout, but just as the rat reached my tin I fired. Uncle Sam leaped to his feet, scared half out of his wits; he was sure that a shell had struck our dugout. When he saw what I had done, he said, "Why in hell don't you take the brutes out when you want to shoot them, and not be making a mess here?" There was only about twelve inches of slush in the dugout at the time. But our favourite method of killing this loathsome animal was to fix our bayonet and, sticking a bit of meat on the end of it, put our rifle over the parapet; then when Mr. Rat came along and nibbled at the meat, we would pull the trigger and the rat would make a hurried exit out of this world—of course we could only do this at night.

During the day our favourite pastime was getting up hot lunches and serving afternoon tea, and most of the soldiers

Jack O'Brien

became expert at this. Our cookstove consisted of an old bully-beef can with holes punched in it. In the bottom of this can we placed several small pieces of gunny sack, and on top of this we put several pieces of trench candles. When the candle melted and ran down over the sacking it produced a good steady blaze and it gave out considerable heat—best of all, it didn't make any smoke, for of course smoke in the front line would be apt to draw shell fire. Over our fire we could boil the full of our mess tin of water and make our tea—also, we could warm up our rations in this way, and meat and vegetables tasted a lot better when they were hot. We also carried Oxo cubes and prepared coffee so we could have a nourishing drink at any time.

Some time on in February preparations were made for a raid on the German trenches. Officers and men consulted together, and the men in charge were busy drawing up plans and perfecting arrangements; we were very much excited over it, and every one hoped that they would be among the fortunate ones chosen to take part in the scrap. The 29th Battalion was holding the line on our right, and they were coming in with us on this. Finally the plans were given out; the raid was to cover about fifteen hundred yards of the enemy trench and the battalion scouts and bombers were the ones chosen to go over. The same number of men went from the 29th, and the trench mortars of each battalion protected the flanks of the attacking party and prevented the Germans in the other parts of the trench coming to the assistance of those attacked. Also, a party of bombers were stationed in the "Glory Hole" ready to act as reinforcements if they were needed—I was one of the latter bunch, and oh how I longed for the signal that would give me a chance to share in the fun!

The attack was planned for 3 A.M. At the sound of a whistle they were to go over the top, enter the enemy trenches, do all the harm they could, and when they heard the second whistle come back, bringing as many prisoners as they possibly could. But before they went out, two men, Conlin and another chap, stole quietly out and cut the enemy's wire entanglements—they lay there for hours right under the noses of the Germans cutting a gap for our boys to go through—I assure you it was ticklish work; the success of the whole enterprise depended on their skilful, silent work. The slightest noise, cough, or sneeze, would mean their own death and the failure of our plans, but nothing happened and they had everything ready at the appointed time.

The boys who were going over had prepared for it as they would for a vaudeville; they all had their faces blackened so they could know one another in the dark, and they were all allowed to arm themselves in any way they wished. Some carried revolvers, others the handles of our entrenching tools (these had small iron cog wheels at one end and they made an excellent shillalah), a few had bombs, and one of the boys, Macpherson was his name, armed himself with the cook's meat axe.

Finally the long looked for moment arrived—the whistle blew and over they went—Lieutenant MacIntyre was in charge of the 28th boys. The wire cutters were the closest and they reached the trenches first—poor Conlin was shot as soon as he showed himself on the edge of the parapet, but MacIntyre got the man who shot him and they fell together. A little farther along the trench Macpherson was lying on the edge of the parapet just ready to jump in when a German came running along the trench shouting "Alarm! Alarm!" Mac leaned over, grabbed him by the shoulder, and said, "Here, sonny, that's a hell of a noise you are making," and with that he brought his meat ax down on his head. The boys were all in now, clearing up the Huns in great shape, and when the whistle sounded the few that were alive were brought back as prisoners.

While this was going on in the German trenches there was great excitement in our own. Our trench mortar was being worked energetically to keep back any German reinforcements. Lieutenant "Spud" Murphy was in charge of this, and his antics kept us all in roars of laughter—he jumped around and "rooted" for those bombs as though they were his favourite players in the National League. When one went over, he would, like the rest of us, jump up on the firing-step to see it light. When it lit fairly in the German trench he would dance around the gunner shouting, "That's a good one!" "That's the way to put them over!" "Now for another beauty! give them hell!"

Well, our raid was a great success, and it was the biggest thing of the kind that had been attempted up to that time. We had a few casualties; Conlin was a great pal of mine, and I missed him the most. Some of our boys were decorated; Conlin, our dead hero, won the D. C. M., and the medal was sent to his people. Lieutenant MacIntyre was awarded the D. S. O., and "Darky" Andrews, who had taken a leading part, also received the D. C. M.

One of the prisoners captured was an under officer, and as he was wounded he was taken to the nearest dressing-station; while his wound was being looked after, an interpreter was talking to him, and the German said triumphantly, "Well, you have brought me here, but you cannot send me over to England." "Oh, indeed!—and why not?" asked the interpreter. "Because Germany controls the water," said our prisoner proudly. "No troops can be brought from England now." "Is that so?" said our interpreter. "Well, sonny, you will find yourself in England by this time tomorrow, however you get there," and he did.

Shortly after this we had several casualties in Platoon 10—two or three were killed, and several wounded and got their "Blighty." Dyer was caught by a sniper, and Tucker was hit in the leg by a machine gun bullet. Quite a few had been wounded in the company and one or two killed, but No. 10 was lucky—we got some reinforcements and to No. 10 came McMurchie, "Fat," and McKone. McMurchie was a little Irishman about five feet tall with a great taste for rum and he didn't know what fear meant. He had a twin brother in another company and they were just like two peas in a pod; only his brother was quiet. Mac would go and line up in his brother's company when rum was being issued and draw his brother's issue, then come back to "C" company and get his own ration, and then line up again and tell the Sergeant-Major that he had given his issue to his brother. He was a proper little devil. One day we were out on rest and Mac had been away all the day before, and this day we were wondering where he had gone, when, lo and behold, into the line of huts marched McMurchie leading a rooster with a piece of string around its neck—he had swiped it off some Frenchwoman—whether he ever took it back I don't know, perhaps the cooks could tell—Mac was pretty friendly with the cooks. He was always getting into trouble when out of the line, but when in the trenches he was worth a dozen men, not to work, but his disregard for all danger made one's hair stand on end. He would do everything one was supposed not to do. He would shave in the front line when Fritz was shelling the trench and everybody else was under cover. He had a big rifle; I don't know where he got it, but it was bigger in the butt than most, and the bore was all worn out; it had been fired so much that when he used to fire it the report was deafening; he used to call it "Big Lizzie." When he was shaving and a shell came close and threw dirt all over him, he would say, "All right, Fritz, wait till I get through, I'll get Big Lizzie after you," and he'd stand up and fire five rounds rapid over at Fritz in broad daylight. Why he didn't get killed was a marvel—when shrapnel was bursting (shrapnel shells are full of lead pellets and when they burst they scatter forward about a hundred yards) he would look at them straight in the face and remark, "That's right, Fritz, lengthen them out a bit." He was out on a working party one day behind the trench, filling sandbags, and there were one or two reinforcements with him, when Fritz started slinging some "Whiz-bangs" over (these are small shells about fifteen pounds full of shrapnel, but they come with an awful speed, that's why they call them "Whiz-bangs," you hear the whiz just about the same time that you hear the bang); well, Fritz was sending quite a few over; I guess he had spotted the party and the new men were kind of nervous. "Aw," says Mac, as he kept on working, "don't bother about those things, there's nothing to 'em but wind and noise—Ow!" and he jumped about a foot as a piece of shrapnel took him in the leg. Mac was absent for awhile down at the Casualty Clearing Station and had his leg fixed up; it wasn't bad. After he had been there awhile the Sergeant asked him to wash the floor; Mac refused, "Do you think I came out here to scrub floors?" says he; "I'm a fighting man." The Sergeant was going to have him pinched, but while he was away Mac sneaked out and came back to the battalion, absolutely refusing to go back, and Colonel Embury, our Colonel, who was a good sport, smoothed matters over and Mac stayed with the boys, and soon was as "right as rain"—he was too tough to hurt. I will leave him for awhile—it would take a book to describe all his tricks—and we will go on to "Fat," who came about the same time. Fat was a big fat good-natured kid, and he and Bink got quite chummy; they were both farmers before the war. Fat had a great dislike for machine gun fire—most of us had too, but Fat was the worst; he also had a comical little laugh—"Tee hee, tee hee" he would go. We used to go out at night stringing wire in "No Man's Land"; every now and again Fritz would sweep the wire with machine gun fire, and directly he started sweeping we would be down like a flash, and wait till Fritz quit. Fat would be in a shell hole almost as soon as the first shot was fired, and would laugh at Bink looking for a hole to hide in. Bink would get sore; all you could hear was the rat-tat-tat of the machine gun and in between "Tee hee, tee hee" from Fat as he lay and watched Bink crawling around looking for a hole. Some of the boys would lie in the hole and wave their legs in the air hoping to get a bullet through them so that they could get back to "Blighty," but they were never lucky enough. We would always lose one or two men on these wiring parties, but we had very few killed and No. 10's luck still held good. By the way perhaps you would like to know why we call England "Blighty"—it seems that it comes from two Hindoo words meaning "My home," and as there were a lot of Indian soldiers out in France at the beginning of the war and they were with the regular English troops, I suppose it was passed along that way—to get a "Blighty" means to get a wound that takes you to "Blighty." To say that a man has got a "Belgique" means that he is dead. The boys have different sayings for everything, and they sound funny unless you know what they mean. "Buckshee" the English troops call anything that you might have to spare, such as "Have you a buckshee razor?" meaning "Have you a spare razor?" The word "buckshee" comes from the Hindoo word "Backsheesh." Well, to continue, the other boy to come to No. 10 was a freak; how the devil he ever got in the Army beats me. He was deaf, and when you spoke to him you had to holler; also, he had a cleft palate so you could hardly understand him when he spoke, but he was a good man in the line and when he was on sentry, he was up on the fire-step looking over all the time; only at night of course. He used to pack along a box of ammunition every night and do his best to fire the lot before morning. When the scouts were out as they used to be every night, patrolling "No Man's Land," the word was passed along in the trench and we would either stop firing or fire high; desultory fire was always kept up all

Jack O'Brien

night. Well, we could never make McKone understand that the scouts were out; and he would keep on blazing away—at last the scouts made a kick and we stopped him firing when they were out—but he was awfully sore. "What am I here for?—I'm not a dummy," said he. One night he had been blazing away and had made Fritz sore, and Fritz had turned about three machine guns on the spot where Mac was. The bullets were coming around him like bees around a hive, but he couldn't hear them. At last he heard something; Corporal Banks was coming along the trench at the time, and Mac stopped him. "Say, Corporal, there's an aeroplane up there somewhere," and he gazed up into the sky. "Come down, you fool, that's machine gun fire," says Banks. We used to have lots of fun "chipping" him, but all he'd reply was "Aw, you go to h——." One night Bink and Bob were out on "a covering" party—their job was to take their rifle and bomb and lie out in front of our men as they were putting out wire in "No Man's Land,"—the idea is to prevent the party from being surprised by the Germans. It was a wet cold night, and so the officer gave them a drink of rum before they went; in fact, they asked him for it. Well, they crawled out and lay down, and I guess the rum gave them some "Dutch" courage, for after the boys had finished their wiring and gone back to the trench, Bink and Bob thought it would be a good scheme to crawl to the German lines and throw their bombs in. So forward they crawled through his wire till they got up close and heard the Fritzies jabbering; the rum had about worked off by this time, and instead of throwing their bombs, they got cold feet and crawled silently back to our lines—I guess it's as well they did, or I wouldn't have their story to tell—they often laughed about it afterwards.

Shortly after this we moved off that front and we took over some trenches from the Imperial troops in the Ypres salient. It was just about the time that the Imperial troops took back the "International" trench to the right of the "Bluff," and it was a much hotter place than the one we were in before; we had to be right on the alert all the time. We were in there a short time and back we went to M—for a rest, and in the meantime the Battle of St. Eloi commenced—it started with the Northumberland Fusiliers ("Fighting Fifth," as they were called) blowing up some mines under the enemy lines and occupying the craters and a trench—they were then relieved by the "Sixth Brigade, Canadians." It was all quiet for awhile and then the storm broke; all the German artillery for miles was concentrated on this front of about a thousand yards, and the men were literally blown out of their positions. It poured rain and our aeroplanes were unable to take observations, with the result that, where at first our artillery was firing too far, when they shortened up, they shelled our own men. The Germans also concentrated heavy trench mortars on the craters, and after blowing the men to pieces all day, they attacked at night. What men were left died where they stood. All the bottoms of the craters were just a pool of thin mud, and when our boys were wounded they just slid down the sides of the craters and perished in the pool of mud at the bottom. Some of the craters were lost, and our relieving parties, going in at night to relieve, what they thought were our men, found the Germans in possession and bomb-fights ensued. In the meantime the enemy artillery had a barrage across behind the craters making it almost impossible for men to get through alive. The 28th were hurried up and after spending a night in "Dickebush" we were taken up to "Scottish" Wood in support. Woodrow, Webster, Corporal Grimsdale, and all the company bombers were sent out from there, and they held one of the craters. After hanging on the lip of the crater all day under a constant rain of "sausages" (one hundred pounds of high explosives in each) they tried to dig in and consolidate, but they had lost half their number, and then the Germans attacked them from all sides. They worked their rifles as long as they could, but they were clogged with mud; and then fought them hand to hand—

those that fell never rose again—slipping down into that horrible mess at the bottom. Webster saw Woodrow fall, and he and Grimsdale fought their way out; Grim happened to find his way to our lines, but Webster got lost and for twenty-four hours, that night and the next day, he lay out there; in the daytime he had to lie still and at night he couldn't find which line was ours; and machine guns were spitting all ways. At last he crawled near our trench and heard the boys talking, and he came in; it was two days after when I saw him—five days before he had been a happy, daredevil sort of a boy—now he looked like a corpse with living eyes of coal. He never got over it, and after the Battle of Hooge was invalided home, a complete wreck. While all this was going on, "C" Company was brought from "Scottish" Wood to the communicating trench, and where we entered the trench was crowded with men, one bunch trying to get up, another stream of wounded coming down. As fast as men tried to get through the barrage, they were wiped out, and at last the officers decided to lose no more. Fritz started to shell the trench we were in, and a lot of the boys were hit; our officer took us out in the open, and we lay there while the trench was being shelled—after staying there twenty-four hours we were relieved—but the struggle for the craters still went on; sometimes our fellows holding them, and sometimes Fritz. At last the weather brightened, allowing us to get observation, and our artillery was able to work accurately; then the battle died down, leaving two craters in the Germans' hands, two in ours, and the rest a sort of "No Man's Land," in which constant fighting took place for months; sometimes quiet, but flaring up again whenever either side tried to take and hold the remaining craters. That was the Battle of St. Eloi as nearly as I can give it. It was the first big scrap we took part in, and although it wasn't a victory, nobody knows, but those who were there, how near we were to disaster, and only individual pluck kept the Germans back; for after the barrage went on, Headquarters could not get news of how things were going. Several officers were sent up, but were either killed or wounded trying to get through the barrage. Those who got through stayed to help those that were there fighting, as it was almost impossible to get back. It was there that the Sixth Brigade got the name "The Iron Sixth." While the company I was in didn't do anything spectacular, I can tell you it was all we wanted, lying out there in the mud and wet, expecting any moment to see the Germans advancing, and all the time shells coming like hail. Some of the companies of the 28th lost heavily—I think we were the luckiest; but when the battalion went back to rest billets a lot of boys' faces were missing that we had been familiar with for months.

Now that heavy fighting had commenced we never knew where we would be for more than a day at a time—we stayed in the lines till there was someone ready to relieve us, whether it was two days or ten—then we went direct to rest billets, and we remained there till we were needed again in the front lines. The billets were not bomb-proof, by any means. They were well within range of the big guns, but after the heavy shelling and bombing in the front lines they seemed like heaven. We had been out there two or three days when little Mac came to me and said, "Say, kid, I'm on the track of a bomb-proof job." I said, "What makes you think that?" "Well," said he, "just as I came down the line I over-heard the old Sergeant telling another guy about it, and if we can get on, will you come?" I said, "You mutt, it all depends on what it is." "Oh, I thought I told you," says Mac, "they are calling for men to go to the tunnellers." "Nothing doing for this child!" "Now, look here," says Mac, "you've only got to die once, and you might better be buried in a sap than be blown to hell by a big shell, there would be more of you left for your friends, anyway, besides a change is as good as a rest, and as there seems to be small chance of us getting any rest, we might just as well keep this chance." So I said, "All right, we can try it for a week, and then if we don't like being buried, we can come back to life; that's more than most people can do"; so away went Mac to tell the Sergeant that we would go. He said, "Well, I'm sorry to lose you boys, but I don't blame you for wanting to get away from what we have been going through lately, and any time you want to come back to the old boys we will only be too glad to have you." He told us to report to a branch of the Royal Engineers known as the 250th Tunnelling Company. They were located in the Kemmil dugouts, so away Mac and I went to old Kemmil, where we had been all the previous winter.

When we reached the line of dugouts we stuck our head into one and asked where we would find the officer in charge. A voice from a far corner called out, "*Oui*, the bleeder is in the end dugout, old cock!" We found the officer's dugout without any trouble and reported for duty. He told us that we would not be needed till night, and that we had better go and find a dugout to rest in, so away we went back to the place where we had inquired for Headquarters. It was our first brush up against the English Tommy, and we were anxious to see more of him. We went into the dugout and found about a dozen men lying around, some of them rolled in their blankets trying to sleep, and others smoking. I went over beside the chap who had answered my first question, and after telling him who I was and what I was there for, he made room for me and I sat down. He was a funny-looking little chap about the build of a wooden toothpick, but he looked as if he was made of steel wire. We soon struck up a conversation, and his "Cockney" sure did sound funny to me; he was one of the sappers, and when he found that I had left the Infantry to join them he was disgusted. "Well," said he, "you are a bloomin' ass. Why, blime me, mite, this here's the worst bleedin' job in the Army; a man digs till the sweat rolls off, and all he gets for it is a bleedin' shilling, and he has to give six-pence of that to the old woman; blime, it doesn't leave ye enough for bacca, and all the fellas think this is a bomb-proof job—why, blime, you dig and sweat for days, and Fritz sends along a blinkin' torpedo and fills up the tunnel, and there's all your hard work gone to 'ell, and you with it too if you 'appen to be around," and believe me I found out that most of what he told me was true, and sapping was no bomb-proof job. Well, we sat around all day enjoying the conversation of our Cockney friends. I found that my new friend was nicknamed "Skinny," and during the next few months he took a great liking to Mac and me, and he stuck around with us most of the time.

That night at 8 o'clock the Sergeant in charge came around and detailed eight of us to go up to the sap,—Mac, Skinny, and I were among those chosen,—so we started off to a place known as "S. P. 13" (Strong Point No. 13). Skinny was in the lead, as he had been there before. We went through about a mile and a half of communicating trench, and there we encountered three or four infantrymen bound for the front lines. The bullets were whizzing over our heads, and once in a while a shell dropped near us, but nothing happened till we had to come up out of the trench and cross an open space. The infantrymen were in the lead, and almost as soon as we struck the open one of them "got it" in the head. Skinny was in front of me, and he stopped so suddenly that I said, "What's wrong, Skinny?" He said, "Blime, but he's got it; I wonder how many blinkin' kids the poor devil's left." The poor lad was killed instantly and we picked him up and laid him on one side with his cap over his face—the stretcher bearers would find him and carry him back of the lines. We continued on our way, and Skinny, paying no more attention to flying bullets than he would to flies, led us to the sap where we were to begin work. At the entrance to this particular sap was an immense shaft leading down 107 feet, and shooting out from this shaft were two main tunnels—these tunnels were four feet high and about three in width, and they ran under "No Man's Land" and past the first line of German trenches, the object being to reach a small wood and lay a mine under some pill-boxes that were causing us a lot of trouble. These pill-boxes were machine gun emplacements made of concrete, and our heavy shells had no effect on them. Our only chance of getting them was to blow them up with a mine. When I went in, there was still quite a distance to go, for the wood lay behind the second line of German trenches.

I was set to work on one of these tunnels, and using pick and shovel seemed mighty hard at first; what made it harder to stand was the lack of fresh air—there was no place for the air to get in excepting through the main shaft, and that was about four hundred yards away. Then too, we could never rest ourselves by standing upright, and the constant bending of the back was torture until we got used to it. However, our shift only lasted for eight hours, and then we went out on rest for twenty-four hours, and our rest billets were three miles back, so they were fairly quiet. Altogether the work was a pleasant change when our muscles got hardened to it; and there was always something interesting turning up. Of course the Germans had their tunnels too, and they were trying to reach our lines. Often we could hear each other working and sometimes one party would send in a torpedo to block the other's tunnel. I remember the first one they sent us. That day I was working at the bottom of the shaft hitching sandbags to the rope by which they were pulled to the top. Skinny was coming down the ladder in the shaft, and when he was about ten feet from the bottom, the torpedo was fired. It just missed our tunnel and the concussion was so great that it gave us a great shaking up. Poor Skinny lost his hold on the ladder and fell into two feet of water. I was scared stiff, for I didn't know what had happened, but when I caught sight of Skinny sitting in the water I just roared. Skinny sat there with his head above water making no attempt to move, but when I laughed he looked up indignantly and said, "Blime, mite, you'd cackle if a fellar broke his bleedin' neck," and then while I continued laughing he cursed the Germans with every variety of oath to which he could lay his tongue, vowing what he was going to do to get even, but all the time sitting there in the water. Finally he came to his senses, and jumping up hurriedly he made a bee-line for the ladder and began to climb. I said, "Where the devil are you going to, Skinny?" He called back: "Do you think I'm such a bleedin' fool as to stay down here and get buried alive? I don't intend to be buried till I'm dead." He urged me to go with him, but I figured that the Germans would expect one torpedo to do the trick and they wouldn't be likely to waste a second one, so instead of going out I went back along the tunnel to see if any damage had been done. I found a little loose earth knocked down—that was all the harm it did, except to give us a good scare.

Our work went steadily on, and gradually our backs got like iron and we didn't mind the everlasting bending. In our twenty-four hours at rest billets we had lots of fun. Mac and I were the only Canadians in the bunch, and 'the' English Tommy used us "white." About this time there was great excitement over some German spies that were supposed to be in our lines, and there was a reward offered of 20 pounds and fourteen days' leave to any one who would succeed in capturing one of these spies. We were all warned to keep a sharp lookout for them, and our own officers were forbidden to go around through the lines without an escort. Several spies were caught masquerading in our uniforms and of course they were shot; a spy stands very little show of getting off if once he is caught, and it is a brave man's job in France. Of course we have our men behind the German lines, and I don't suppose any one will ever know all that our secret service has done for us there.

Jack O'Brien

We were all keeping a sharp lookout, and one night one of the boys caught a German trying to crawl through our front lines, he made him prisoner, and maybe he wasn't elated over his capture, so he marched him proudly down through the long line of trench to our Headquarters; but, on getting there, imagine his surprise when his German prisoner began to talk and joke with the officers; he was one of our own secret service men and was just returning from a trip through the German lines—he thought it was too good a joke to miss, so he let himself be captured. I had heard all this, and I made up my mind not to be fooled, but one night I thought sure I had the real thing. Mac, Skinny, and I were coming off shift at 2 A.M., and in the communication trench we met an officer without an escort. We saluted as we passed, and he said, "Good-night, boys." Mac whispered, "I believe he's a spy." Skinny said, "Blime, I believe he is too." We talked it over about fifteen minutes and then we decided to follow him, so we gave chase and caught up with him just outside a line of huts where there was a sentry posted; when we came up he was talking and laughing with the sentry, so we stood in the background and listened, and what do you think—if that guy wasn't the officer in charge of the guard, so our fourteen days' leave and our 20 pounds was all shot in the head—that cured my spy catching.

When on rest we were billeted in some of the little villages behind the lines, and we struck up quite an acquaintance with the French peasants living there. "Old Madame" was a particular friend of ours, and we got to know her best because she made her living by serving lunches to the soldiers; she had a nickname for each of us, and if any one was missing she had to hear all about it. Many a pleasant evening we spent in her little home. A bunch of us would go together, and we would take along our mandolin, banjo, and mouth organ, and have a little concert; Madame would sit there and smile, not understanding a word we said, but enjoying seeing us having a good time—another thing, it was always warm there, and that was something that our billets never were.

But we had a great time trying to get enough French so that we could ask for what we wanted to eat and many laughable incidents occurred in our struggles to make Madame understand. For instance, one night Skinny wanted eggs, and he tried in every way to make his wants known, but Madame failed to get his meaning, and finally the boy got desperate, so jumping up, he started to run around the room cackling like a hen. He got the eggs all right, and I think he earned them; but it was so funny that we nearly rolled off our chairs laughing.

To make things better, a party of twenty-five Canadians came to the tunnellers and we had some good old times together; but Mac and Skinny were still my best pals; many's the prank we played together. One of our favourite ones was to work the officer in charge for an extra ration of rum. The British Tommy was given his ration of rum as soon as he came up from the sap, but we Canadians had to wait for ours till we reached our rest billets, and it was served to us there by one of our own officers. The only exception made was in favour of those who had been working in a wet part of the sap; for instance, at the bottom of the shaft there was often two feet of water, and at various places along the tunnel where we had struck springs the water almost flooded us out; it kept two pumps going all the time to make the place dry enough to work in. Well, the men on these pumps (two on each) and the one at the shaft were served out with rubber boots and oilskins, and these were the only Canadians who received their ration of rum from the Imperial officer. Usually one of our trio was chosen to work on either of these wet jobs, and he would line up for his rum ration—after getting it, he would hurry out and hand over his oilskins to one of us, and we would slip them on and take our place in the line—after we had been served we did the same trick, and usually the three of us succeeded in getting our extra ration of rum. Of course the officer would catch on after awhile and would chase us out, but we worked it on every new officer. It wasn't that we cared so much for the rum, but it was the fun of getting something that we were not supposed to have. It was the same with our money ration— we were only allowed fifteen francs every two weeks while we were in France, and the rest of our pay was *kept for us* by the military. Now, fifteen francs did not begin to get us what we thought we needed, and many's the scheme we tried to get at the balance. Finally we hit on one that worked pretty well. Mac made over "so much a month" to the family of one of the English boys in the 28th, they cashed the cheque and forwarded the money to their boy, and he handed it over to Mac; we were having a "whale of a time" on his extra money, and one day we were expecting our remittance from England. Mac met some battalion boys who told him that Sergeant Banks had the money for him; little Mac was on a carrying party that night when he met the boys, and he hurried back to tell me the good news. I was working above the shaft, and Mac and I sat in the shelter of an old wall, and with the bullets buzzing around us we planned how we would spend that money. Finally we thought we had lost enough time, so I went back to work and Mac started down "Suicide Road" for another load of sandbags and planks for the tunnel. He had about a mile to go, and the road he was on got its name from the fierce shelling that Fritzie gave it every night. If you have ever been out in a bad hailstorm you can perhaps form some idea of how thick the bullets are when Fritzie turns on his guns and sweeps a road. Well, I had only been working an hour or so underground when I heard some one at the top of the shaft calling my name. I answered and he said, "Come on up, Jack, I want you." I hurried up the ladder and found one of the 28th boys waiting for me. I said, "Hello! what's the matter, old chap?" He said, "Jack, little

Mac's got it." "Little Mac, oh no, not little Mac!" I cried. "Why, he was here with me only a little while ago." "Yes, I know," he said; "he was on his way back with the first load when it got him—still, he isn't badly hit, and he sure did act funny when he got it. This is how it happened: we were walking down the road with our loads when Mac stopped suddenly and said, 'Boys, I believe I'm hit; I felt a stinging pain go through my leg.' He felt around and walked a few steps, and said, 'No, I guess I'm all right. But, gee, it was a close call!' He hadn't gone far when he felt something trickling down his leg, and slipping his hand inside his trousers he moved it around the spot where the pain had been, then he pulled it out and held it up; it was covered with blood. As soon as he saw the blood Mac grabbed his leg and limped like everything. He dropped his load right there and made a bee-line for the dressing station. As he hobbled down the road he called, 'Good-bye, boys, it's Blighty for mine.'" Of course I laughed at what the boy told me of little Mac, but all the time I felt an ache in my heart, for something told me I would never see my brave little pal again, and I never did. He did not get a "Blighty" after all, but was sent to our base hospital at Le Havre. When he came back to the lines I was gone, and he went back to the battalion; he "went west" from Vimy Ridge, where so many of our brave boys fell.

Well, I hunted up Skinny and told him about Mac, and when the shift was over and we started off to our rest billets we both felt mighty blue; if we had known that we were to be separated the very next day we would have felt still worse. But that's one thing that's good about the Army—you never know what's coming, and after it has happened there is no spare time for regrets. When I said "Good-bye" to Skinny, he said, "It's a bleedin' shime that you 'arve to go, mite. Those bloomin' 'Eadquarter blokes doesn't know what they're doin' 'arf the time. It's blinkin' 'ard to lose both you and Mac, but 'up the line with the best of luck,' old cock." But I must explain why I had to go. An order came asking all Canadians who were working with the Royal Engineers (which was an Imperial unit) to transfer at once to the Canadian Engineers at Ypres. This did not sound very good to us, as the Ypres salient was known as a pretty hot place. However, as military rules say, "Obey first and complain afterwards," there was nothing for us to do but go. We were sorry, also, to leave before the completion of our mine at Kemmil—but we heard afterwards that when it was set off it turned the wood literally upside down. When we arrived at Ypres we found things very different to what they were at Kemmil—instead of mine laying we were put into a protection sap; this was only twenty feet down and consisted of a network of tunnels for the protection of our own lines against the German sappers. My first duty was on "listening-post" in one of these tunnels, the hole where I was being just large enough to lie in, and it seemed almost like being buried alive. Here I did not get my twenty-four hours' rest as at Kemmil, but I worked on a six-hour shift and had only ten hours off; even then we were not sent back to rest billets, but had to stay in the dugout at the top of the shaft. At the end of seven days we were supposed to be sent back to rest billets, and another shift would take our place. Fritzie had been unusually quiet since we came, and we began to think that the stories we heard were greatly exaggerated.

However, on the morning of the seventh day we changed our minds. We had gone to work at eight o'clock feeling unusually good—we expected to be relieved at seven that night, and we had been promised a seven days' leave to Blighty, so I could hardly wait for the day to pass. Instead of being put on "listening-post" this morning, the Corporal in charge took me with him—we went down a long tunnel till we reached the end, and the Corporal put a listening-tube to his ear; he listened a few minutes, and then handed it to me and whispered, "Do you hear anything?" I said, "Yes, I hear some one shovelling." He said, "I heard them yesterday, and I think they are close enough for us to get now, we will lay a torpedo for them here," so we got to work to dig a place for our torpedo, and after working for half an hour or so our candles went out. Then we noticed that the number of shells falling above us had greatly increased—we lit our candles again, but it was no use—there seemed to be a terrific bombardment on and the concussion was so great that we could not keep our lights going. Fritzie was certainly making up for lost time. The Corporal said, "Well, Jack, we might just as well go up and see what is doing," so we started back to the shaft; our candles were out, so we had to grope our way along. We had not gone far when we heard some one calling for help. Following the sound, we came to a hunch of men belonging to the infantry; they had come down for protection from the shell fire, and a shell had blown in the entrance to their tunnel. Not being used to the network of tunnels, they were completely lost. We guided them out to the main shaft, and it was still intact, so they went up; then the Corporal said, "I wonder if there are any more back there?" I said, "I don't know, but I think we had better have a look," so we went back and after searching every tunnel and not finding any one, we decided to go out ourselves, and we started back along the shaft. We were feeling our way along with the shells dropping overhead like hail, when all at once two "Krupps" landed on the tunnel just over my head; there was a terrific explosion, the props of the tunnel gave way, and in another instant I found myself choked with dust and half buried under a pile of dirt. The Corporal was crawling along three or four yards ahead, and in the darkness he could not see what had happened. As soon as I could get my breath I yelled, "Hey! Corporal, come back." He said, "What's the matter?" I said, "By golly! I have half of Belgium on my back." So he came back and pulled me out,—my back was badly strained, but otherwise I was none the worse,—but we both realized now that things up above must be getting pretty serious, and once more we started for the shaft. The Corporal was ahead, and he called out, "Say, Jack, we are in the devil of a fix now!" I said, "What's up?" He said, "Those confounded Boches have blown in the top of our sap-head." This was a serious matter, for it meant cutting off our supply of air as well as our chance for escape—it would be bad enough to be killed in a fair fight, but we didn't relish being buried alive; however, we would not give up without a struggle, and we began searching the nearby tunnels for a shovel. In the darkness I heard some one moving, and I said, "Who's there?" A familiar voice said, "Who in hell do you think it is?" I said, "Nobby! is that you? What the mischief are you doing?" He said, "I'm looking for what you never can find when you need it, a d—shovel." The lad was one of our tunnellers, and we were glad to have his company and also his help in the "digging-out" process. Not finding a shovel, we commenced work with our hands—after we had been working for half an hour Nobby grabbed me and whispered, "Do you see those lights?"—I turned around, and there, about fifty yards away and coming towards us, were about a dozen lights. We talked it over with the Corporal and decided they must be Germans who had broken through the tunnel, so the Corporal said, "One of you boys stay here and dig; and the other two will go back and stop them," but we made him stay, and Nobby and I went to meet the Bodies. There was a branch tunnel about thirty yards away, and we hoped to waylay them there; we were armed with revolvers and their lights made them good targets. We reached the branch tunnel just before they did, and we had a lively little scrap with the first two—the others put out their lights when they heard the pistol shots—anyway, they were several yards back and they were in no hurry to get into the fun. We lay there and waited for them, and after things had been quiet for a few minutes they lit their lights and came on—fortunately the tunnel was only wide enough for one man, but all the same we were looking for a lively time—they were ten yards away when there came an awful explosion; a shell had burst directly over their heads. All I remember was a blinding cloud of dust and a gust of wind as our tunnel was blown in, and once more I was buried. We scrambled out and turned to look for our foes, but they had received the full force of the blow and were safely buried; so we thanked our lucky stars and went back to our digging. When we reached our Corporal, we found that he had already dug his way out into the shaft. We crawled out, and looking up we discovered three more boys at the top of the shaft—these belonged to the machine gun crew who had taken up their position there, but a heavy shell had demolished their gun and buried the men—they were just digging themselves out when we appeared, and we gave them quite a surprise. One of them said when he saw us, "Well, where the devil did you come from?" I suppose he thought that because we came from below we must have some connection with his Satanic Majesty. Well, we climbed up to where the boys were and gave them a hand at the digging; finally we made a hole large enough to let in a little air and then we all lay down and rested. We were almost dead for want of air, for we had been buried for four hours, and we did not know what might await us once we got out. After we rested up a little, we finished our digging and crawled out. We found ourselves in a large shell hole, the former trench being blown away. The ground was being swept by machine guns and heavy shells, and it was not healthy to rubber around very much. There was an officer in charge of the machine gun crew, and finally he found a spot where there was a slight protection, and he took a look around and this is what he saw; the line of trenches we had left there in the morning were entirely blotted, and the ground, as far as he could see, was literally riddled with shell holes. Our boys had either been killed, wounded, or taken prisoners, and our first and second lines were in the hands of the Germans; however, their advance had been checked, and now, before going any farther, let me explain that this is

Jack O'Brien

known now as the Third Battle of Ypres, and the history is familiar to all. It was here that the 1st Division of Canadians made their heroic stand in 1915, just one year previous. But to come back to our present plight. We were at a loss to know what to do, for we had no means of knowing how far the Germans had penetrated our lines; but we knew that if their first wave of reinforcements ever came up, they would surely get us, so there seemed to be just one thing to do, and that was to make a dash for our supports—the Germans who had come over were taking what shelter they could in the shell holes, but they were lying as low as possible, on account of the fierceness of our shell fire. It really seemed as though every gun we had was trained on that spot, and the fire was coming from three sides. One of the 28th boys who was watching the battle from a neighbouring hill said that more shells fell to the minute in this battle than in any he had ever seen, and certainly that is the way it seemed to us; there was just one chance in a thousand of our getting through, but the idea of staying and giving ourselves up never entered our heads.

It took quite a bit of courage to make the first dash, but at 2.30 we started out over the shell-swept ground. The shell holes were only from ten to twenty feet apart, but I assure you it seemed quite far enough. We made a quick sprint for the first one and landed in on the backs of three or four Germans; they were lying facing our lines, and hadn't expected any one from the rear. We had them finished before they got over their surprise and none of us were hurt in this scrap—so we made a bolt for the next hole. However, we were not so lucky this time, and before we reached the hole two of our boys went down; we dared not stop to see how badly they were hurt, but plunged into the shelter of the hole. Here we were outnumbered two to one, but our attack from the rear gave us the advantage; still it came near being my finish, for my revolver jammed, and a big Boche made a lunge at me with his bayonet—I dropped my revolver, escaped his bayonet by making a quick side-step, grabbed his rifle, and hung on for dear life. We rocked to and fro, and all at once it occurred to me to use my feet—so I lifted one foot and let him have it right in the stomach. He let go his hold on the rifle and sat down as suddenly as if he was shot, while I lost my balance and went sprawling in the other direction. I don't know which of us would have recovered first, but one of our boys settled the combat by blowing the big Boche's head off. Our three lads had cleared up all the others and we had time to think of our own condition. We were a very sorry-looking outfit; we all had wounds and bruises which we hadn't felt at the time they were received; our tunics and caps had been left in the sap, and the few clothes we had on were torn and plastered with mud, our faces were streaked with dirt and blood, and we were "all in." I hadn't known any of the boys before except the Corporal and Nobby, and poor Nobby was the first one shot. Well, we looked after each other's wounds, and then we rested for awhile; when our strength came back a little, we started out again. We would have stayed longer only we had no idea how far we were from our lines, and we felt sure that German reinforcements would come up at dark. We went out in single file and not too close together, but our next hole was farther away and just before the first one reached it a shell burst directly over it; two of the boys were killed and the Germans in the hole were blown to atoms; the officer and myself were thrown a little distance and badly stunned, but finally we managed to reach the hole. We were the only ones left, and we lay there bruised and shaken. We were pretty well discouraged over the loss of our other brave lads, and it was quite a while before we felt like venturing out again; the only redeeming feature was the fact that the shell which had killed our boys had also cleared the hole of whole Germans. Well, at last we made another start, and we had almost reached a hole when the officer, who was behind me, shouted "Look out, lad, there's another coming!" We leaped for the hole and landed at the bottom only to find ourselves covered by a dozen German rifles; I sure thought I had a through ticket for the next world with no "stop-overs" allowed, especially when I noticed a big "square-head" in the act of bringing a "potato-masher" (hand grenade) down on my head. I dodged him as he fetched it down, and just then the German officer in charge of the bunch bawled out some command. They all lowered their rifles and began talking in an excited manner, they were evidently trying to decide what to do with us, and the officer said, "Well, I guess our game is up, boy." I said, "I guess it is"; and really I didn't much care if they finished me right then. I knew I had made them pay the price anyway—we were out of ammunition and, besides, we were too much "all in" to put up any kind of a scrap.

Well, they evidently decided to take us prisoners, for we were searched, and then two of them were detailed to take us back—the only reason we were spared was because it is quite a feather in a German's cap to take a British officer prisoner—they are always rewarded for it. Well, they started us out at once over the same road we had come, and we went from shell hole to shell hole as before, but now that we were under German escort no one "potted" us, and in spite of the shell fire we reached what had been "No Man's Land." As we crossed this I noticed a funny thing. A company of German reinforcements were being brought up, perhaps a hundred in all; the officer in charge was bareheaded, and he carried a revolver and a stick of some kind. Instead of leading his men as our officers do, he walked behind and a little to one side, really on their flank. They couldn't hear his commands and he tried to show them where to go by pointing with his stick, but he kept his revolver levelled on the men all the time. As I watched them, a couple of our "Big Lizzie" shells burst right over them; when the smoke cleared away there wasn't one of the bunch to be seen. Well, we crossed "No Man's Land" and came to where the German trenches had been, but they were as level as our own. Finally we struck a communication trench and the going was a little safer. The trench was crowded with Germans, and they lined up in either side to let us pass. But here I had another narrow escape; the Boche's hatred of the British is such that they cannot resist giving vent to it when they have one in their power, and as we passed one big brute made a lunge at me with his bayonet. Fortunately, he missed his aim a little and the bayonet passed through the loose front of my shirt, but I felt the cold steel on my flesh—the guard said nothing to him. Another thing I noticed on my way out was the treatment a wounded German received from the comrade who was taking him out—the man was wounded through the head and he was evidently dizzy from pain and weakness, for he rolled from one side of the trench to the other like a drunken man—instead of carrying him as our men would do, or, at least, putting an arm round him to steady his steps, that brute walked behind, and when the wounded man would stop, wanting to sit down and rest, I saw the brute take that poor man by the collar, jerk him up, and land him a couple of kicks. This of course sent the man running and sprawling down the trench, and this is the way they made their way out.

Well, we went on till we came to a German strong point, and here we found fifteen of our boys that had been captured earlier in the day; when we came on the scene they were being photographed by the Germans. The Germans allow their soldiers to carry cameras and almost every soldier has one; we had at least a dozen levelled at us that day—they were evidently taking pictures to send back to Germany— "Prisoners *we* have captured" would no doubt be the title.

They kept us hanging around here for half an hour, still under our own shell fire, and then we were marched back about three miles. Our first stop was beside an old Belgian

Jack O'Brien

church, and here we were taken over by an escort of Prussian Lancers, and for the first time I realized that I was really a German prisoner. We were herded together like a flock of sheep and driven ahead of our captors; we were made to go ten miles before they allowed us to stop, but to add variety to our otherwise tedious march, when our escort wanted a little fun they would put spurs to their horses and ride pellmell through our little bunch. It was great sport to see us dash in all directions tumbling over one another in our efforts to escape being trodden down by the horses; no wonder they laughed and shouted in their glee! And it was on a par with other things they did on that trip. We passed through several small Belgian villages, and when the Belgian women saw us coming, they ran out with jugs of water, chocolate, and cigarettes, but our escort met them and refused to allow them to give us anything. They were very plucky, and some of them dashed in past the guards, and these inhuman beasts known as Prussian Guards levelled their lances and made at the girls. Sometimes they missed; a water jug carried by one of the girls saved her, but I saw three women run through the body by these devils, and all because they wished to do an act of kindness to men who were wounded. The first thing we do with our prisoners is to feed them and dress their wounds, but these are the last things a German thinks of doing. Well, the same thing happened in all the villages, only we warned the girls away when we saw how they would be treated. I also noticed that the Belgians were not allowed on the sidewalk when a German was passing; if they did not get off, they were knocked off.

Finally we were halted in one of the villages and herded into a filthy horse stable. There were about thirty in the bunch and most of us were wounded; we had not even had a drink since we were captured, so we were pretty much "all in." We slept on the floor of the stable that night, and next morning some German guards came along and picked us up. For breakfast we were thrown four loaves of German bread and a pail of water was set inside the door. After breakfast we were lined up on the street, and a German officer who spoke a little English came along and asked us questions. He took our name and number and also the name of the unit to which we belonged. He said he was doing this so that he might report our capture to the military authorities in London, but he had another reason. After he got through he chose two from each unit, lined them up, and marched them off to a large building. I happened to be one of the number. The building where we were taken was occupied by a German general and his staff. We were put in a small room and two at a time marched out for an interview.

The first ones taken belonged to a machine gun crew; they were conducted into a long room at the far end of which sat the General and two interpreters. Along each side of the room was a line of Prussian Guards. The officer who had charge of the boys could speak English fairly well, and instead of taking them to where the General was, he sat down with them at a small table just inside the door. He appeared very friendly, and offered them cigars, cigarettes, and wine. The boys were cute enough to know why they were offered wine, and they "declined with thanks" but they took the smokes. The officer asked them questions about Canada and appeared very much interested in our country, he talked for half an hour and never mentioned war; then he asked them to go up to where the General was sitting. On the table in front of the General was a map of the front line trenches, and through the interpreter the General proceeded to pump the boys for information. This is a sample of the questions he asked them:

Interpreter: "Show me, on the map, the position your machine gun was holding on the Ypres salient."

Jack O'Brien

Boy: "I am sorry, Sir, but I can't read a map."

He asked him several more questions of a similar nature and received unsatisfactory replies. Then he said, "Now, give me an idea of how many guns were holding the Ypres salient." The lad thought for a minute and then said, "Sir, as near as I could guess, it was about a million and a half." The General let a roar out of him like a mad lion, and two of the Prussian Guards grabbed the boys and, dragging them to the end of the room, threw them out of the door and down the short flight of steps at the entrance. I saw them pass the door of the room where I was sitting, and said, "Hully gee! what the Sam Hill are they doing with those chaps?" Sandy said, "Evidently they are not wanted in there." But the boys didn't seem to be at all displeased over the treatment they received, for they landed laughing, and as we went in I heard one say, "We slipped one over them that time, eh?"

A young Scotchman and myself were the next ones called, and we represented the sappers. The same officer brought us in and treated us as he did the first two; we helped ourselves to the cigars and cigarettes, but did not think it wise to touch the wine (Scotty said afterwards that it was the only time in his life he ever refused a drink). After having a smoke, we were taken up before the General. Scotty was a comical chap, very ready-witted, and we had arranged that he should do all the talking. The first question asked was, "Where was the sap you were working in?" Scotty looked up very stupidly, and said, "I don't understand you, Sir." The interpreter said, "Where was the mine you dug underground?"

Scotty: "Oh yes, I did that for a living before I joined the Army."

Interpreter: "Then show me on this map where the sap was."

Scotty: "I don't know of any sap in the front line."

Interpreter: "But you said you belonged to the miners!"

Scotty: "Yes, but I was not working on a mine in the front line."

Interpreter: "Then what were you doing?"

Scotty: "Well, it was like this; I was only in the trenches twice, the first time our Corporal put me on a fatigue party and I was carrying up sandbags and rations."

Interpreter: "Is that all you did?"

Scotty: "Yes, Sir."

Interpreter: "Then what were you working at the second time you were in the lines?—you were surely put in a sap this time."

I could see that both the General and the interpreter were getting quite peeved, but Scotty answered smilingly: "I will tell you what I did. The Sergeant in charge gave me a long stick with a nail in the end, and I had this stick in one hand and a sandbag in the other, and my work was to go through the trenches picking up all the paper, cigarette boxes, and tin cans." When this speech was interpreted to the General, the old boy was *wild*. I think he would gladly have put an end to us right there, but he only shouted an order to the guards, and we were hustled to the door and kicked out. When we picked ourselves up, we sat down on the steps and had a good laugh. Evidently the General was not satisfied with the information he received, for none of the others were taken in. We were all taken back to the stable and left there till the next morning, then we were marched off to the railway station and loaded on a train for Germany.

We travelled in cattle and box cars, and we did not sit up to see the sights because all of us were wounded or injured in some way. My back was badly strained when I was buried in the sap and I was bruised from head to foot. I had had nothing to eat all day excepting the small piece of black bread given to us in the morning. It was about 9 P.M. when we made our first stop in Germany, and this was at a large prison camp near Dulmen, Westphalia. Dulmen is a beautiful large city; and the camp is two miles out. At first sight a prison camp looks very much like a chicken ranch; the high wire fences around the whole enclosure and the little frame huts in the centre all carry out the idea. But when you get in, there is a vast difference, the outside fence is fourteen feet high, and of barb-wire with the barbs poisoned; three yards in, there is another fence, a low one this time, to prevent the "chickens" getting under, and this is made of live wire. In between these fences there is a line of German guards, each one having his own beat. The centre of the camp is divided into small blocks, each with its fourteen-foot fence of poisoned wire; there are six huts in each block and about fifty prisoners quartered in each hut. When I was there the camp contained about three thousand prisoners—French, Russian, English, and a few Canadians. But, to go back to my arrival. As we were marched into the camp we were a pretty sorry-looking lot. The old prisoners saw us coming, and rushed back to their huts and brought us out some food. The new prisoners were not allowed to mingle with the old ones until they had been two months in camp—I suppose this was to prevent any news getting in—so in order to do anything for us, the old prisoners had to catch us on our way through. Well, they brought us, from the contents of their Red Cross parcels, hardtack, biscuits, bully-beef, and jam, and when we reached our hut we had a pretty good meal. The boys had none too much for themselves and it meant a great deal to give up any of their precious food; but they knew, from experience, that we were starving, and we thought we were, for after good army rations, one small slice of black bread does not go far towards satisfying hunger. But, after existing on German fare for two months, we knew what it was to be really hungry; we were more like famished wolves than human beings.

This is a day's ration, served out to us the first day in camp, and in the two months I was there it never varied: for breakfast, a small bowl of coffee made from dried acorns, and served without milk or sugar. It was so bitter as to be almost undrinkable, and there was not one morsel of food given with it. For dinner we were allowed a bowl of stuff they called soup. It was made by boiling cabbage and turnips with a few dog bones; when I went there first I wouldn't believe the boys when they told me that our soup was made of dog bones, but one day I met one of the French prisoners who had been a doctor, and we went for a walk around the grounds, so I asked him what kind of an animal went into our soup and he told me it was just ordinary dog. We argued the question for several minutes, and I was still unconvinced, so he said, "Go into the cook house and see for yourself." I went, and the cook (who was a French prisoner) very obligingly lifted out some bones with his long spoon and showed me one of Fido's legs. That settled the question, and, naturally, I enjoyed the soup more than ever. As an extra treat, to give it a special flavour, sometimes they threw in the bark. The boys had taken their own way of finding out what they were eating—they saved all the bones for several days and then they put them together—the result was a German Dachshund. We had nothing but this soup for dinner, and for supper we were given a bowl of slop which the boys called "sand-storm," and a three-pound loaf of Deutschland black bread to be divided among ten of us. This bread was made from ground vegetables mixed with rye flour. If you read

Gerard's "Four Years in Germany" you will see that samples of this food were examined by a specialist and declared to be almost devoid of food value. It was planned to reduce our numbers by a process of slow starvation.

We used to fight over the garbage cans for the peelings of potatoes, and cabbage, and when the old prisoners, who were getting their Red Cross boxes, brought us their German issue of soup, it was not safe for them to come inside our enclosure. They would place the can inside the gate and we fought over it like a pack of hungry wolves. If you think we are exaggerating, see Gerard's new picture film "My Four Years in Germany." It tells better than I can just how bad things were. Well, one day when our soup was handed in by the other prisoners a funny thing happened; we had seen the boys coming and had made a rush to the huts to get our bowls—a very short fellow reached the soup can first and before he could get his bowl filled, we had all crowded in on top of him—poor Shorty had his head and arm in the soup and was almost drowned before we got him out. He had soup everywhere except in the bowl. Every British prisoner had to put up with this kind of food for the first two months; after that, the Red Cross parcels would begin to arrive. The condition of the Russian prisoners was indeed pitiable. They received no help from home, and were depending solely on German food. A Russian can live on much less than a Britisher, but they literally starved to death on what the Germans gave them. They were made to work, and when they could go no longer and fell down from sheer weakness the Guard would beat them till they died. I have seen this happen again and again, and there was an average of fifteen deaths every day among the Russians alone. Our parcels came just in time to save the strongest of us, but scores of the weaker ones died. But just here let me explain the system used by the Red Cross for getting food to the boys in the prison camps. As soon as a new prisoner reaches the camp he is given a card which he fills in and sends to the Red Cross Headquarters in London. This card contains his name and number, and the number of the camp that he is in. It takes about two months to get the first parcel through; after that he received six food parcels and two of tobacco each month, and once in six months they send him a complete outfit of clothes, from overcoat to boots, also a parcel of toilet articles, such as toothbrush, shaving outfit, soap, etc. From the time these parcels reach the Dutch border, they are handled by a staff of our own prisoners, so there is no danger of their going astray. The Germans examine the parcels before they are given out to make sure that they do not contain maps or compasses for the prisoners; that is the only time they handle them.

These parcels mean life and a small degree of comfort to the boys, so you can imagine how they are looked forward to. The Red Cross saved my life and the lives of thousands of our boys; and they deserve honour and support from every person who calls himself a loyal citizen of any Allied country. I shall never forget when my first parcel came; I had been in camp two months and I had failed eighteen pounds. One of the boys came into my hut and told me there were two parcels for me. I told him to stop fooling, that his joke was stale. But he said, "No, it's straight goods this time, here are the tickets"—so I rushed off to where the parcel office was and got in line. Pretty soon my turn came and I handed in my tickets. A big German brought out the parcels, and while he was censoring them I was figuring on what I was going to have to eat, but imagine my disappointment when he pushed over the parcels and I found they contained nothing but clothing. There were two suits of underwear, two pairs of socks, two shirts and one pair of blankets, but no food. My clothing was in rags when I reached Germany, my tunic and cap were lost in the sap the day I was taken, and I needed socks and underwear very badly, also boots, so this

Jack O'Brien

supply was more than welcome, but I needed food more than anything else. I put all the stuff into the blankets and started back for the hut. When the boys saw me coming, they rushed out to meet me, for they were building on a feed, the same as myself. The unwritten rule of the prison camp is, whatever one gets the rest all share it, so they were disappointed too. However, three days later our food parcels arrived, having been delayed at the border, and we sure had a big feed. My first food parcel contained one tin of Welsh rarebit, one tin of jam, a large package of biscuits, three bars of chocolate, and two packages of cigarettes. I tell you it put new life into us, and we felt like licking all the Huns in sight.

After our Red Cross parcels came we were able to shave ourselves, and we had soap to wash with. When we first came to the camp the Germans asked if there were any barbers in our bunch. Now, there wasn't, but one of the boys, "Slim" Evans, volunteered for the job. They gave him an old razor, some soap and a strop, also a small brush, and he was ready for work. He had no chair of any kind, so he looked around till he found a bench in one of the huts; he swiped this and turned it upside down on his table. When the boys came for a shave, they climbed up on the table and sat in the upturned bench, using the leg of the bench for a head rest. It sure was some "barber's chair"; I'll bet there never was another like it. Well, Slim got lots of customers; the Germans didn't pay him for his work, but the prisoners tried to. Some had nothing at all, but he did their work just the same; others were working on farms, and for this they were given what was equal to 2d or 4d in English money. Slim never took anything from those who only received 2d, but those getting 4d were allowed to pay. Sometimes they gave him a box of German cigarettes so strong that if you smoked one on Monday you could taste it on Saturday. I remember my first visit to Slim; I climbed up into the chair and Slim asked me what I was getting; I said 4d, so he gave the razor an extra rub-up. Now, I hadn't had a shave for a month, so I was a pretty hairy-looking customer. Slim said, "How long since you've had a wash?" I said, "This morning, only I hadn't any soap." He said, "Never mind, I'll wash you with shaving soap." So he went to work, and really I didn't know whether he was shaving or skinning me. As a matter of fact he did a little of both, for he had six patches of skin off when he finished and the only remark he made was, "This razor is not quite as sharp as I could wish," but he told me to be sure and come again.

But I have spoken mostly of food, or rather the lack of it. Now I will try and give you an idea of how we put in our time. They didn't work us very hard in this camp; usually we were only taken out three times a week. When they wanted us, German guards would come in, line up about twenty of us, and take us out to work in the fields. The first job they put us at was planting potatoes and we worked faithfully the first day, but when we came in that night I said to "Snipe," the new pal I had made, "By golly! Snipe, I don't like the idea of producing food for these 'square-heads,' let's see if we can't put one over them." "All right," said Snipe, "I'm game, but how in hell are you going to do it?" I said, "Well, how would this do? Next time we are sent out, I'll take the hoe and you the bucket of potatoes; as soon as we get a little piece away from the guard, I'll keep on making holes, but you just go through the motions of dropping in potatoes, then when we reach the centre of the field I'll make an extra large hole and you can dump in all the potatoes except a few that must be saved for the other end of the row." "Gee, that sounds all right," said Snipe; "we'll have a try at it anyway, and I believe it will work." The field we had been working in was a long narrow strip containing about five acres, and there was an armed guard stationed at each end. Well, next day we were called out again and we tried our new plan. It worked splendidly; the other boys saw what we were doing and they all did the same, so the whole field was planted that way, and I wish you could have seen those potatoes when they came up.

The next thing we were given to do was putting out cabbage plants (of course they had not yet discovered the trick we had played with the potatoes). In planting cabbages the first man was given a small sharp stick instead of a hoe, and man number two had a box of young plants. A hole was made, but before the plant was put in the roots were nipped off. In three days the cabbages were all wilted or dead and the Germans could not make out what was wrong, so they sprinkled the ground with some kind of stuff thinking the damage was caused by worms in the soil. But some one happened to pull up a plant, and they realized then what had been done. Of course they were very angry, but no one would tell who did it, and they couldn't very well punish the whole camp. However, they didn't give us any more farm work to do.

Shortly after this, I was out on a working party with some of the old prisoners and one of them began telling me about a man who had made an escape from the camp some months before. He had gotten as far as the Holland Border, but was caught there. The word "escape" thrilled me as nothing else ever had, and from that time on the idea was never out of my head. I questioned the man and got all he knew about the distance to the border, direction, etc., and I could hardly wait till night to get telling the other boys about it. Finally we got back to the bunkhouse and I told Snipe and two or three other Canadians what I had heard. They were just as excited as I was, and we decided that if that fellow could get out of the camp, why we could too, and we made up our minds to keep working on it till we did find a way out.

One night when we were discussing the question, Snipe

suggested that we cut a hole through the floor of the hut and tunnel our way out. We could make the hole under one of the bunks so it would not be easily seen by the guards. The plan seemed good to us and we began immediately to put it into operation. Snipe happened to be occupying one of the lower bunks, so we started there to cut the hole in the floor—we had only a couple of old jack-knives to work with—but after we got through the floor, we did the digging with our hands. While two of us worked the other lay on the top bunk where we had a small window, and kept watch. The floor of the shack in which we lived was two and a half feet from the ground, so there was plenty of room for the earth that we took out of the tunnel. We worked away for eight nights and by that time we had passed the inner fence, the guard and the electric wires, so we thought it was safe to come to the surface. When we got within a foot of the top we decided it was too late to attempt to get away that night, so planned to start at 11.30 the following night and that would give us time to get quite a distance away from the camp before daylight. So we went back to our bunks, and all that night we lay planning and dreaming of what we would do when we got out.

Next morning I was too excited to sleep, so very early I got up and took a walk around the fence. When I reached the place I thought our tunnel should be I took a look in that direction, and to my horror, I discovered a big hole between the two fences. I knew in an instant what had happened: when the Germans were changing guards, their weight had broken through the tunnel—I smile now as I think of the surprise it must have given them, but at the time it was a bitter disappointment. I hustled back to tell the boys, and Snipe moved into another bunk so that they couldn't fasten the blame on him. Of course we knew that the tunnel would be traced to our hut, and sure enough in about half an hour a bunch of guards came in, lined us up, and tried to make us tell what ones had attempted to escape. We all denied it, so after making a thorough search of the hut for maps and compasses they let us go. Thus ended my first attempt at escape.

Shortly after this the guard came in one morning, lined up about fifty of us, and said they were taking us away to work on farms. We were taken to the railway station, loaded on trains, and taken farther into Germany. When the train stopped and we got out, we found that we were in the centre of a coal mine district. With their usual regard for the truth they had taken us to work in the coal mines instead of on farms, and this mine where we were was well known among the prisoners of war as the "Black Hole of Germany" and it has maintained its evil reputation up to the present time.

The other camp we were in was a paradise in comparison with this. Owing to the fact that the train came up to the mines, there were no wire fences except just in the centre where the prisoners' huts were located. But there seemed to be guards everywhere. The first thing that struck us was the dirt of everything, the smoke of the coke ovens covered the whole place with a layer of soot.

It was five o'clock in the evening when we arrived, and we were this time turned loose with the other prisoners; there must have been five hundred at this camp—Russian, French, and English. We were the first Canadians to go there.

We found the barracks and every other place in a filthy condition, the beds were dirty and crawling with the largest fleas I have ever seen; these fleas are as large as ordinary mosquitos, they breed in the mine and are carried up on the men's clothes. Often these pests were so bad that the men lay out in the yard at night instead of going to bed—anyway, in the hot weather the stench from the beds is almost unbearable.

We walked out among the prisoners, and they were glad to get news of the war and of the outside world. Among other questions, they asked if London was still standing. The Germans had told them it had been levelled to the ground. Some of the men had been in the mines for two years and the stories they told were almost incredible. The Germans who guard this camp are always savage and cruel and they are urged on by the owners and operators of the mine. We talked with some of the first British prisoners who arrived there, and this is what they told us: At first they refused to work, knowing that it was contrary to international law to force prisoners of war to work in the mines. For refusing to work they were given a week of the most brutal abuse and torture possible. The weather was bitterly cold and there was a foot of snow. These men were stripped of everything but their shirt and pants and made to stand "at attention" out of doors. Any man moving hand or foot was knocked down with the butt of a rifle, and those who fainted from cold and exhaustion were dragged away and put back in their places as soon as they became conscious—while those whose strength enabled them to hold out the longest were stood in front of the cokery ovens until they were utterly exhausted by the terrific heat, and had to consent to work. The first shift that went down into the mines were driven into the cage with rifle butts and bayonets, and some of them went down unconscious. Oh, when this war is over, there will be a long day of reckoning with the German people.

After listening to such stories as these, and after seeing the poor wrecked bodies of the prisoners, you can imagine how we felt as we were marched off to work the next morning. When we were taken out, we were given our first suit of prison clothes—this consisted of overalls and smock and

Jack O'Brien

cap. The overalls had a four-inch stripe of red down each leg, the jacket had six inches of red down the centre of the back, and the cap had a wide red band across the top. After we got into these, we looked like a bunch of robins.

When we reached the pit-head we found a line of German civilians waiting to go down into the mines—as we waited for the cages to come up we overheard some of their conversation—of course we could not understand it, but one of the old prisoners translated it for me. The Germans had noticed that we were new men and they asked the guard what nationality we were. The guard told them we were Canadians, but the civilians said, "Oh nix! the Canadians are 'Swas'"—meaning black. They argued with the guard for fifteen minutes and then were not convinced. Finally the cage came, we were loaded in, and it started down. I shall never forget the feeling I had; I thought that we would never strike bottom. I asked an old prisoner how deep the mine was, and he said two thousand feet, and I believed him.

Well, at last the cage reached the bottom and I had my first view of a coal mine; even to my inexperienced eye things seemed to be in very bad shape. Owing to the great demand for coal, they did not take time to properly timber their mine, and the tunnels were caving in all the time—I am safe in saying that there was an average of three men killed there every week. There was never an inquiry made into these deaths.

Well, they started me to work and my job was to load up cars with the coal that the civilians hacked out. These cars held just a ton, and I had to push the loaded car onto the main tunnel or road; an engine took it the rest of the way. This was very heavy work, and often I thought my back would surely break, and it hurt me to think that the Germans were getting so much out of me. However, as the days went on we found little ways of getting back at them. For instance, the civilians were paid according to the number of tons they got out, and each man had tags with his number on them. When a car was loaded we were supposed to put one of these tags on the top, and when it reached the top of the shaft it was credited to the man whose number was on it. Well, sometimes, instead of putting the tag on the top of the load, we put it inside and piled the coal on it. At the top of the shaft, when no tag was found, the car was not credited to any one, and when pay day came and those old Germans found the paymaster did not give them credit for all the coal taken out, there surely was some fun; it did our hearts good to hear the row they made. Of course we would not have been able to play any tricks if there had been any guards around, but once we were down in the mine we were out from under military rule and working under the mine management, but the latter were just as cruel in their way as the military; they not only got every ounce of work possible out of each prisoner, but they inflicted the most terrible punishment for every slight offence. A few days after I went there, a splendid young Canadian boy from Toronto was found dead with the back of his head smashed in. He had been on night shift, and he had not been hurt in a cave-in, for our own boys found him. We asked for an investigation, but we were told to go to work and mind our own business; so we Canadians went on strike. A German who spoke a little English asked us what was the matter, and we said we wanted to find out what had killed our comrade. He laughed in our faces and said, "You are prisoners, you must do as you are told." We told him where he could go, and against the advice of all the old prisoners refused to go to work, and this was our punishment; we were stood "at attention" in fifteen-minute periods, with five minutes "at ease," until ready to go back to work. This was indeed torture—the five minutes' rest made it possible to prolong the agony. Men faint if made to stand "at attention" for many hours, but doing it this way we never lost consciousness.

Jack O'Brien

Guards marched up and down behind us; if we moved hand or foot we were knocked down and kicked; though they kicked us on the ankles whether we moved or not—my right ankle was so swollen I was not able to do up my boot for three weeks. Well, we stood this without food for two days and nights, and then we were so exhausted that we had to give in. The old prisoners had all been through this kind of thing, that was why they warned us not to go on strike. But no matter what the punishment was, we could not let the murder of one of our number go unnoticed.

Shortly after this we had another lesson of the same kind. An Englishman on night shift was found sleeping and the foreman who found him knocked him down a shaft and killed him. Another Britisher, who saw the murder, reported the foreman, and accused him of the murder, but when the trial came off the Britisher was given six months in prison for perjury.

But to go back to our work. We were supposed to be on eight-hour shifts—only sometimes they would make us do a double shift, or sixteen hours. When this was required they gave us an extra bread ration. The German in charge of the camp thought himself very smart because he could speak a few words of English and also write a little; so, instead of telling us that we were to come to his office for an extra ration of bread, he wrote the order on a piece of cardboard and hung it in our barracks. Seeing him hanging something up we all gathered round, and this is what we read: "You Englishmen, before going on shift, will draw your *Breath* at my office." Of course we all shouted and laughed at this; and the officer stood there looking as though he had been kicked and didn't know who had done it. He tumbled that there was something wrong with the notice, but all he said was "You Englaender, Schweinhunds," and went out.

It was while we were working on one of these long shifts that we thought of another way of getting even with our slave-drivers, for this is really what they were. They worked us to the last ounce of our strength; the food given us was not sufficient to keep body and soul together. We were living on our Red Cross parcels, and we ate none of the German food except the bread. It's the only time I ever worked for nothing and boarded myself. We were punished for every offence, real and imaginary, and when a man is driven harder than he can bear, and refuses to work any more, the methods used to force him to work would put any slave-driver to shame; and we were ready to do anything to try and even up the score. This is one plan that worked well.

There was a great deal of rock among the coal, and we were supposed to have two cars always on hand, and fill one with rock and the other with coal; but we thought as nature had mixed them in the mine that they should go up the same way, so we would half fill a car with stones, and then cover it over with coal. When this car reached the top it looked all right, so it was put into the dumping machine; once there it could not be stopped, and when those big rocks went rolling down into the machinery and over the sieves, there was one hell of a smash-up. Those old Germans would tear their hair with rage, but of course they couldn't tell who had done it. Finally, like everything else that went wrong, it was blamed on the "Englaenders," as we were called, and the old German who spoke English took the case in hand. One night, after coming off shift, he lined us up and said, "I have been notified that you Englanders are putting stones in between the coal, and if I hear any more of this you shall be punished *severely*." Some one started to laugh and we all took it up, so he stood us "at attention." No matter what was done to us we never gave them the satisfaction of letting them know it hurt. I have seen our boys die under slow torture, and always they had that *grin* on their faces.

This was one thing the Germans never could understand, for, as a nation, they have no spirit at all; I have seen big men blubber like children over the slightest hurt. Working with civilians, we often had the satisfaction of a scrap. We dared not touch one of the military, no matter what they said or did, for it would mean instant death; but when the civilians were extra-brutal or insulting, as they often were, we got even if we did not happen to be too greatly out-numbered. The smallest Britisher that ever went into the mine could lick the biggest Hun in a fair fight. But that was just the trouble— the Germans know nothing about the first principles of fair play. At school, instead of being taught to defend themselves with their fists, they fight with sticks or anything they can lay their hands on, and once they get their opponent down, they kick him until he gives in. So when they ran up against English-speaking people and there was a scrap in sight, they were astounded to see the Englander lay down the shovel or whatever he happened to have in his hands. They would stand and stare with their weapon half raised as they saw their opponent laying aside his only means of defence. They did not know what to expect, and while they were in this uncertain condition the Englander got in his first blow. We became quite notorious for our methods of fighting, and when we would be put to work with any new men, their first question would be, "What did you do before joining the Army?" and we always said, "We were boxers." They would smile and say, "Ich nix boxer—nice Englaender, good Englaender"—this amused us immensely and their fear of us made them use us more decently.

After I had been in the mine about six months, Snipe and I planned out a scheme by which we hoped to escape doing any work for awhile. In going through the mine, we had come across many abandoned tunnels from which the coal had been taken—in many cases these tunnels were partially caved in and were considered unsafe, and for this reason they were avoided by the miners. The idea came to us this way;—one night when Snipe and I were coming off work, we passed these tunnels, and I said to Snipe, "Say, old boy, I'm fed up with this everlasting work for these brutal Huns; let's think up some scheme for getting out of it for awhile." Snipe said, "All right. But how can we get away from these blamed 'square-heads'?" Just then we noticed one of the tunnels, and I said, "Hully gee! Snipe, what's the matter with hiding in one of these tunnels? No one ever comes here." "Golly! I believe it would work," says Snipe, pounding me on the back. We were very much excited, and when we reached our bunkhouse we told some of the other boys. They asked to come in too, so six of us laid our plans. We went down on shift as usual and followed the other miners till we came to the tunnel in which we had planned to hide. When there was no one looking, we would dodge in, and when we were missed the miners thought we had gone to work in another part of the mine; each mine boss thought we were taken to work for some one else, so no one hunted us up; of course we were in constant danger of being buried alive, but we gladly took the risk for the sake of getting a rest.

We would lie round chatting and sleeping all day, and at night, blacken our faces and join the other miners on their way to the main shaft. We worked this game for eight weeks, not always staying in the same hole, but changing around whenever we saw a likely looking place. We had a splendid rest, and it put us in better condition for what was to follow. A funny thing happened after this had been going on a few weeks. One morning two of our boys, Barney and Raeside, did not come down in the same cage with us, and as we didn't dare wait, for fear of being set to work, we were out of sight before they arrived. So they hunted up a place for themselves, and the spot they chose was between the timbers and the roof of the main tunnel. It was a good place, and they would never have been discovered if they hadn't gone to

Jack O'Brien

sleep and snored. But they did, and a fire boss happened to be passing at the time, so he located their hiding-place. Of course he couldn't see who was there, but he tried to poke them out with his stick. They soon woke up, but Barney whispered, "To hell with him, Mac, we won't go," so they lay still. Finally the fire boss went for help, and as soon as he left the boys came out. But they had to come out one at a time. Barney got down first; and he beat it to locate another hole. When Raeside struck the tunnel, he saw a light not far away, and he thought it must be the returning boss, so off he went in the opposite direction. Barney had the light, and was looking for a place large enough to hold them, when he heard Raeside running. He at once jumped to the conclusion that Raeside had spotted a "square-head"—and he started off to his assistance—Raeside heard some one coming on the run, and he thought it must be the boss, so he went still faster. They chased each other like this for about a mile. Then Raeside gave out: and hiding his lamp, he hid in the first hole he came to. In a moment along came Barney, puffing and blowing like a whale, and as he passed Raeside saw who it was. Then the joke of it struck him, he called Barney back, and the two of them sat down in the tunnel and laughed till they were sore. The boss never found them, and I can imagine how angry he was when he went back with his reinforcements and found his prey gone. That night the boys told us the joke they had played on themselves.

But our good time ended abruptly one Saturday when a mine inspector, or "fire-stager" as he is called, came around on his tour of inspection, and he found us hiding in a hole about three hundred yards from the main road. We put out our pit lamps when we saw him passing, and he didn't let on having seen us, so we couldn't tell whether he had or not. He was too big a coward to tackle us alone, and we knew that if he had discovered us he would go for help. We didn't know whether to run or risk staying where we were, and while we were talking about it, we heard the tramping of a lot of feet in the tunnel leading to our hiding-place. It was too late to go now, we would have to face the music. There were six of us, and Snipe suggested that if no more than ten came we would stand and fight, but if there were more we had best make a running fight and escape to some other part of the mine. We decided to do this, and while we were waiting for them to come in we filled our pockets with stones.

But the foreman had no intention of bringing his men in—he lined them up, ten on a side, opposite the hole through which we must come out—they were armed with sticks, pieces of heavy rubber hose, and anything they could lay their hands on. After lining them up he made them hide their lamps under the jackets so that we wouldn't be able to see them when we came out. Then, when he got them fixed to his liking, he very bravely marched in where we were and said, "Alle Englaender?" We said, "Yes." He said, "You Schweinhunds!" At that one of our boys jumped and made a pass at him, crying, "You big square-headed German, I'll knock your head off, I wouldn't take that from your Kaiser Bill." The German backed up and avoided the blow, saying tauntingly, "Ah, nix, Englaender." Then he asked us why we were not working, and we said we had got tired and were taking a rest. He said "Komm' mit." We said, "Oh no." When he saw we had no intention of going he began to make promises. He said that if we would only go back to work he would not report us and we would not be punished in any way.

We did not believe him, and we trusted his promises about as long as it took him to make them; but, as Snipe said, we might as well take a chance on it, for we had to get out, and there was only one road to go. Of course he couldn't understand us, but we had picked up enough German to make out everything he said. Well, we pretended to believe him and we started out, walking in couples. When the first two reached the main road two lights flashed out, and the clubs commenced to whistle through the air. The boys shouted "duck!"—and, believe me, we did. We started down between those two lines of Germans, and seeing there were so many we thought it best just to make a run for it. In going through, three of our boys got knocked down, and the rest of us got some bad whacks over the head and back but we kept our feet. The last two Germans on the line got scared when they heard us coming and started to run. They were on the road just ahead of us, and we made a dash after them. They were a considerable distance from the main body when we overtook them, and I remember one of the boys saying, "We'll make these square-headed devils pay for what we've received"— and believe me, we did. Instead of going home to their supper that night, I'll bet they went to the doctor.

Well, when this scrap was all over and we got to the top of the shaft, the mine inspector that had caught us reported us to the military authorities, and their punishment was five hours "at attention." When we had put this in, they allowed us to go to our bunks. The next day was Sunday, and we were peacefully sleeping when a big German came in and called out our numbers. We asked him what he wanted, and he said we had to go on the Coke-o-roy. We certainly knew what this meant.

The coke ovens were attached to the mine, and most of the coal taken out was made into coke. Work on the ovens was so hard and so trying on account of the great heat, that they used this as a punishment for anything that was done wrong in the mines. This is what the German who could speak English told us. The morning we were put on, he lined us up and read this to us, "If you Englaenders does not do your work right beneath the mine, we put you on coke ovens, and there, if you shall not work, you shall die." We all laughed at this, and he said, "You England Schweinhunds!" and went away.

But it was sure a punishment. The regular hours through the week was a twelve-hour shift, and each man was obliged to shovel thirty-two tons of coke, wheel it from ten to twenty yards along the platform, and dump it into railway cars. On Sunday the shift was twenty-four hours long, and each one had to handle sixty-four tons of coke. If you were not through when your time was up, you must keep at it till you did the required number of tons and then start back to work again with your shift.

It was on the twenty-four-hour shift that we started our work. We went on at 7 A.M. on Sunday, and we worked from that until 7 Monday morning. Almost as soon as I went on the ovens I met two of my old pals, Nickelson and Macdonald. They had been put here for attempting to escape from the mine, and had been at this job for a week before we arrived. We were mighty glad to see each other, for we all belonged to the same "school." But a "school" in a German prison camp does not mean the same as it does in America. We got the idea from the British Tommy, only he calls it "mucking it." It is made up of a bunch of boys who put all their parcels in together and go fifty-fifty on everything. Sharing with each other brought us a little closer together than we otherwise would have been.

Well, these were in our little "school" and had also shared in our rest-cure up to the time of their attempted escape. So when they saw us come on the ovens, they knew exactly what had happened. As I passed Nick, he said, "Which would you rather do, Jack, work on the coke oven or go to church?" I laughed and said, "Well, I guess, the church has it this time." After awhile I happened to be beside Mac, and I said, "Speaking of baseball, Mac, do they serve afternoon tea here?" He said, "Well, they used to, but you know tea has gone up, and as a substitute they serve out a little hell." And believe me, I hadn't been there long before I found that this was literally true.

I was feeling fairly fit after my two months' rest; and this rest was all that saved my life. But during that first day I didn't mind the work so much, I could stand it anyway, but when night came it was awful beyond description. The heat of the closed ovens was bad enough, but at night, when the coke in the ovens was sufficiently baked, they opened the huge doors and the burning mass was pushed out by machinery. It came out a solid lump just the shape of the oven, and the heat it threw off was terrific. Two or three big "square-heads" stood near with iron forks fourteen feet long, and with these they prodded the mass until it broke into pieces. When it first broke it burst into flames, but gradually it cooled, and finally they finished it by turning the water hose on it. But the Germans who attended to this looked like skeletons—the gas and heat seemed to have eaten the flesh from their bones and they seemed scarcely human. I was working near and the fumes of gas and the awful heat was almost more than a human being could stand. I looked around at the prisoners; and such a sight—they were toiling like galley slaves, their faces were streaked with soot and sweat till you couldn't tell whether they were black or white. I'll never forget the horror of that first night on the ovens, I was almost dead long before I had finished shovelling my sixty-four tons of coke, but the awfulness of the scene was harder to bear than the pain of my body. I said to Mac, "What does this remind you of, Mac?" He said, "Jack, it's more like hell than anything that was ever imagined or painted."

We were almost insensible when at last our work was finished; but we had to keep at it as long as our brains were strong enough to force our bodies to move. I saw what the weaker ones got, and that was enough for me. Those inhuman devils with their boasted German culture—a disgrace to everything that God has created—would drag these poor quivering, fainting creatures, pleading for mercy—right up to those red-hot ovens, and at the point of a bayonet force them to stand in that withering heat till they fell unconscious. Then the guard would drag them away and make two of the other prisoners carry them back to the barracks.

What I have described is a sample of what my days and nights were like on the coke ovens, till I made my final escape two months later. I played out several times, and each time I was roasted alive before the ovens. Once I backed away to escape the heat, and the guard knocked me unconscious with his rifle. The strongest men are being crippled and broken down in health in this work (of course the weak ones die very soon), but the treatment accorded our prisoners in other places is not much better. A young lad belonging to the Gordon Highlanders told me that he was wounded when he was taken prisoner, and he lay in the hospital for three days before they even looked at his leg. Then, when he finally got attention, everything was done in the roughest kind of way, and when the nurse had finished the dressing she *spit in his face.*

Another man who belonged to the Irish Fusiliers told me that when he was captured they kept him four days in the front lines doing fatigue duty under our shell fire, and in that time he had scarcely anything to eat. On the fourth night he and three other prisoners were quartered in a small room of a Belgian house, and they were taken down and lined up against the wall, while the German officers amused themselves by pelting them with green apples. One of the prisoners attempted to eat one of the apples and was beaten almost to death.

What we endured was the special torture that was reserved for Camp K 47; they had different methods at other camps. I remember an old prisoner telling me of the torture they had where he was before coming to the mines. It was an ammunition factory, and they had taken a bunch of English prisoners there and tried to make them work. Now, this is where our men drew the line, and though they knew it would mean punishment, and perhaps death, they absolutely refused to go to work. Of course the German officials were raging, and they resorted to their special line of torture to compel obedience. The boys were taken to where boxes were placed against large trees, they were forced to mount these and extend their arms full length about their heads. Then their wrists were strapped together and fastened to the tree—the box was kicked away and they hung by their arms often for hours. Every little while an officer would go around and ask them if they were ready to go to work. On their refusing he would give them a few kicks and pass on. This was kept up as long as the men could stand the agony, and the prisoner who told me this showed me the marks on his wrists, and said he knew at least six of their boys who died as a result of this torture.

The only thing that kept them from killing the prisoners outright was the fact that all the German prison camps were visited every few weeks by American Ambassador Gerard or some of his staff. He passed around among the boys, asked questions, and received complaints, and it is undoubtedly true that Ambassador Gerard saved hundreds of lives in the prison camps.

I had been working on the ovens for something like a month when a fresh bunch of prisoners were brought up from the mine. They had followed our example and were caught taking a rest. With this group was a young Canadian called Toby, and he was certainly "some boy." He was only eighteen at the time, really just a kid, but he had spirit enough for two ordinary men. They put him shovelling coke, and he got along all right till he finished the dump he was working on. Then, after the large chunks were gone, the dust and cleanings should have been put into wheelbarrows and taken over to a crusher. Toby had not been told this, and naturally he loaded it all into the cars. The boss caught him at it, and he stormed and shook his ugly fist in Toby's face. But Toby had learned to take a good deal, so he paid no attention. But the German manager had seen him too, so he came up when the boss had finished, and of course he could afford to be more insulting than his inferior. So after ranting for several minutes and wiggling his finger under Toby's nose he finished up by giving the lad a couple of brutal kicks with his iron-shod boots. This was more than Toby's spirit could stand, and Toby wheeled around and landed him a blow on the jaw; the man staggered back, and before he could recover Toby gave him another that sent him sprawling. The platform boss saw it all, and drawing his revolver he threatened to shoot, but Toby defied him and dared him to go ahead. The bully was afraid to do it, and he contented himself with reporting the case to the guard. Of course the guard came up, and with a great show of force dragged the youngster to the coke ovens and made him stand "at attention." But he hadn't been there long when lunch time came, and as they dared not leave him alone Toby was marched off to the platform with the other prisoners. During lunch he told me about the scrap he had gotten into, and I warned him to be on his guard—I knew the kind of brutes he was up against and I felt sure that they would try to get even if they could get him at a disadvantage. We were drinking pop at the time, and I made him hide the empty bottle under his jacket to use as a weapon in case he was attacked. Well, we went on duty again and Toby was put before the ovens to finish his punishment, but he had only been there a few minutes when the boss came along with a shovel on his shoulder and made Toby understand that he was to go to work under the long platform which held the ovens. So he marched Toby down the stairs and into the darkness under the platform. Suddenly Toby felt his arms gripped from behind and strong hands pinned them to his side, while out of the darkness in front loomed up the burly figure of the manager. He carried a short whip and this he proceeded to lay on to poor Toby, any place at all that he could hit. The lad wriggled with all his might, and finally succeeded in getting his arms free; then grabbing the whip in his left hand, he planted the manager one between the eyes with his right, and down he went. Then, quick as a cat, he wheeled on the other German, smashing at him with his pop bottle. The man tried to protect his face, but Toby's rage gave him the strength of madness, and the first blow broke the German's arm. Toby followed this up with another, and this time gave him a beauty just over the eye. He went down as if he was shot, and Toby started to walk away. By this time the manager had come to a little, and he called on Toby to "Halt!" but Toby paid no attention and the manager fired two shots after him. What he had been through possibly affected his aim; at any rate, he missed and Toby walked quietly back to his place and began work again. The Germans were too proud to let their comrades know how the lad had beaten them up, so they contented themselves with reporting him privately to the guard and giving him seven days' close confinement. Next day, as I passed the prison, I called and asked him how he was, and he said, "Fine! I could beat up half a dozen more 'square-heads' if I had them here; this is better than working on a coke oven, anyway." After Toby got out of jail the boys gave him a great ovation. They cheered him, carried him round on their arms, and fed him with everything they could lay their hands on. Nothing could keep down a boy with a spirit like his, and he made his escape about two months after I did. He was to have come with me, but had a sore foot, so we had to leave him behind.

Poor kid, it's the only time I ever saw tears in his eyes.

The only redeeming feature of my work on the coke ovens was that I was out of doors and could get a glimpse of the surrounding country. Spring had come, and the fine weather made me long for freedom.

Three of us got together one night and figured out a way of escape; one chap known as Blackie, another called Sammy, and myself. Now, as I said before we worked in shifts, one week at night, the next during the day. It was during the night shift that we planned to get away; but there were two things we needed badly—namely, a map and a compass. We were talking this thing over one night when Sammy said, "I have a scheme." We told him to get it off his chest. "Well," he said, "I think I know where I can get a map and a compass; I work with a German civilian whom I think could be easily bribed." Blackie said, "What makes you think so?" Sammy answered, "I have worked with this fellow for three nights, and I have been treating him to some of my lunch, and he seems to be pretty hungry." Then he said, "We will all save food from our next parcel issue—chocolate, bully-beef, and biscuits—and I will take them and see what I can get for them." We all agreed, but we hadn't much hope of getting what we wanted. In two days along came a parcel issue and we saved out all we could spare and handed it over to Sammy. Next day Sammy took it with him, but brought it back when he came from work. When I saw him I said, "No luck, Sammy." He said, "Sure—come here and I'll tell you all about it." He said, "I got him going fine, and he'll bring the map and compass tomorrow." "Then, why did you bring back the food?" "Oh," he said, "I just showed it to him, and his eyes stuck out a mile," but I said, "No, Fritzie, this is for you when you bring the map and compass; so I think I have him." Sure enough, Sammy went off the next day with his little bag of rations. About two hours after we got started to

Jack O'Brien

work Sammy came along to where I was working and said, "Jack, I have it." We wanted to have a look at it right then, for it seemed too good to be true, but when we were looking at it we were nearly caught by one of our guards who happened to be passing. We curbed our curiosity, and did not bring out our treasures again until we were safe in our huts.

Every night we pored over our map and laid plans for our escape the following week when we would be put on night shift; but before the week was up I was put on a different job. Instead of shovelling coke I was set to filling small cars with coal. This took me away from the boys, and at first I was very much discouraged. But the new place where I worked was a large coal shed and quite dark; right at the back I found an unused door which was unlocked. Opening it, I discovered an iron ladder leading to the ground, and I said to myself, "This is just the chance we've been looking for." That night I told the boys of my find, and they said, "Yes, but how are we going to get there?" for between this coal house and the platform where the boys worked was a distance of one hundred yards. But I told them how I thought it could be managed, and we made our plans to try it that way.

We planned to make our "getaway" on the Tuesday of the following week, so we set about collecting provisions for our journey. All our pals were willing to contribute, and they gave us bully-beef and biscuits from their scanty stores. We could hardly wait for the time set for our starting, but at last the night came.

Every night at twelve o'clock the guards left their posts and marched the prisoners back to a hut for lunch. It was on our way back from this lunch that we hoped to get away. The guards always left us at the foot of the stairs leading up to the coke ovens, and they stayed at the foot of the ladder until the last prisoner was mounted. This night we had made up our minds that we should be the first ones up the ladder, for time meant everything to us. A guard was stationed at the foot of the ladder leading from the coal shed, and we had to make the distance before he did. Our path lay past the coke ovens, across a bridge to the coal house, through it and down the ladder. We didn't dare run, for we were surrounded by German civilians, but I assure you the time we made wasn't slow.

Blackie and Sammy came with me instead of stopping at their ovens, and we trusted to the friendly darkness to keep them from being detected. We won our race and reached the bottom of the ladder a full minute before the guard reached his post; so we were off on the run for a small wood which was about six hundred yards away. We reached it in safety and congratulated each other on our escape. We stayed there only long enough to get our wind, then we started off at a good brisk walk; as far as we knew we had not been missed, for there was no pursuit. We walked until 4 A.M. across the country, then we came to a large wood where we hid for the day.

Next night we started out about 9 P.M., and after a short walk we came to a large river. By consulting our map, we found it was the River Lippe, and we scouted along its banks in search of something to take us across. Unfortunately there was no boat in sight, and just when we had made up our minds to swim it I discovered an old bridge. It had been condemned and was no longer in use, but we were only too glad to try it; crawling carefully across in case there should be a guard at the other end. Just as we reached the centre we encountered a barbed wire entanglement. This made us feel quite at home, and we fancied we were back in the trenches. By the time we got through the wire, our clothes were in rags, but nothing could dampen our spirits, not even the rain that was falling, now that we were really getting away. We reached the end of the bridge in safety and found that it was not guarded, so we kept right on. The first thing we knew we came in sight of a village, and as it lay right in our way we decided to risk going through it. It was 2 A.M., and we marched through the main street of the town and not even a dog barked. We continued marching as long as it was dark, and just at daybreak we were fortunate enough to come to a small forest. It had been planted, and there were roads on every side; and although it was only three miles from a large military training camp, we decided to risk the day there.

We were very tired and two of us slept while the other kept watch. About 10 A.M. we were awakened by the sound of music, and on investigation found that a German battalion was coming our way. My heart was in my mouth as they came nearer and nearer, and I dreaded lest they might stop for a rest. They came within fifty yards of our hiding-place, and we could hear the officer's commands: "Right—left—right—left," but to our intense relief they passed us by. Just as they passed we heard the order given, "Alle singen," for the German troops do not sing because they feel like it but because they are commanded to. I had found this out from a German civilian who worked beside me in the mines.

All that day people passed up and down the roads, and we had some narrow escapes. One man came swinging along through the bush, and he passed within ten yards of us. We thought that day would never end, and longed for night and the friendly darkness. It was 10 P.M. before it was safe for us to leave our cover, but at last we were on the tramp again. About 2 A.M. we came in sight of the big prison camp at Dulmen. It was only about one and a half miles from us, and we could see the sentries making their rounds on the outskirts. We had all been there when we first entered Germany, so it looked quite familiar; but still I cannot say we had any desire to get back.

Travelling on, we came to a large swamp, and had either to wade through or go six miles round. We decided on the former plan, and soon were up to our waists in water. It was early in May and the nights were still very cold, and the water was like ice; but there was nothing to do but go through, now that we were wet, and as Blackie said, "It was bad luck to turn back." For two hours we waded, and at last, chilled to the bone, we reached the other side. Here we found ourselves in a farming district, and we looked eagerly for a safe warm place to hide in for the day. A deserted-looking building off by itself caught our eye, and it proved to be an implement shed with a small quantity of hay in the loft. This looked good to us, and taking off our wet clothes we buried ourselves in the hay. After a good sleep and our daily ration of one biscuit and a small piece of bully-beef, we felt better but still very hungry. All round us German farmers were working in their fields, but fortunately none of them came near us, and that day we had a good rest.

Night came on and we started out once more; this was our fourth night. About midnight we came to a farmhouse, and Blackie asked us how we would like a chicken. We said, "It would look good to us," and so we proceeded to hunt one up. Leaving Sammy on guard, Blackie and I made a tour of all the outbuildings, but there was no sign or sound of a chicken. We were about to give up when we noticed a small building at the end of the house. We went around one side, but failed to find an entrance; and coming to the end of the building, we turned the corner, when all at once a terrific howl arose, and our hair stood on end. Blackie had stepped on a big dog that was chained to the house. We did not wait to make the acquaintance of our newly found friend, but threw ourselves over fences, making the best time possible. The dog barked furiously and we ran half a mile before we felt safe to stop and get our breath. We kept to the roads for the remainder of the night and made good time. We struck some bush coming up to morning, and it looked so quiet that we decided to lay up there for the day. Nothing happened that day, and our greatest trouble was a growing hunger.

Night came, and we were all excited, for this was our fifth night and we judged that we were close to the Holland border. As soon as darkness fell we made our way cautiously out, and after a short walk, came in sight of a good-sized town. Our map showed two towns, one on either side of the border, but as the map was not scaled, we could not tell which one was on the border. As near as we could figure, the German town was a night's travelling from the border, and we decided we couldn't make the Holland town that night, so we took the first cover we came to and laid up for the day. Everything seemed very quiet, and the only disturbance came from some wild birds on a slough nearby.

We had come to the end of our rations. The day before we had only one biscuit among the three of us, and we were in a quandary to know how to divide it. It was hardtack and it would neither break nor cut; so finally we marked it off into thirds with a pencil and each one ate up to his line. We had nothing for a morning meal, and as we lay there, thinking how hungry we were, Blackie surprised us by taking from his pocket a small tin of cocoa. He had been keeping it for emergency rations, and we almost ate him in our joy at seeing anything eatable. The can was quickly opened, and the three of us proceeded to munch down dry cocoa. It stuck in our throats and we looked like greedy chickens that had taken pieces larger than they could swallow. We finished our tin of cocoa and everything seemed so quiet that we thought it might be safe to get up and try to warm our feet. So we each chose a large tree and, keeping behind it, we stamped around in our endeavour to work up a circulation. We had only been at this a few minutes, when to our great astonishment a voice behind us said "Guten Morgen!" We wheeled around and found ourselves covered by a double-barrelled shotgun. It was in the hands of a military policeman who was guarding the border. There was no use resisting, and our feelings are better imagined than described as we were marched back to the nearest town. It was two miles away, and in all that distance he kept us covered every second. I said to Blackie, "Gee, I wish this son of a gun would take his gun off us for a minute," and Blackie said, "No chance of his risking that, but I'm afraid that the crazy nut will pull those triggers, the way he is trembling," so we had to march along, not knowing what minute we would be shot in the back.

Reaching the town, which we found to be Stadtlohn, we were handed over to the military staff, and to our amazement the officer pulled a paper out of his desk and read out our names: Blacklock, Woods, and O'Brien. It was evident that word had been sent to the border towns warning them to be on the lookout for us. Even after we got into the room that fool M. P. kept us covered with his gun, and being in the presence of his superior officer made him more nervous, and his hand shook worse than ever. With six other men in the room, he wasn't in much danger of losing his six hundred marks. One of the boys said, "Isn't that fool ever going to put down his gun?" and the officer must have understood what he meant, for he gave a command in German, and the man not only put down his weapon, but he took out the shells. We breathed easier after that. The officer in charge asked the policeman where he caught us, and he answered, "Twenty minutes' walk from the Holland border." This was the hardest blow of all, for we could have made it easily had we only known. Well, they searched us, and yet they failed to find our map and compass. These were hidden in a knitted belt made for me by one of our prisoners. It contained a secret pocket, the entrance to which was carefully concealed.

Not finding anything, we were lodged in the town jail, and there we stayed until the following day. We were almost starved, but all we had was a piece of bread and a bowl of soup.

Next morning two guards came to take us back to the mine— we went by train and arrived about 6 P.M. Of course they gave us a warm reception. As soon as we entered the gates we were met by German boots—*with feet inside*—and in this way were escorted to our quarters. Once there we were made to stand "at attention" for seven hours, with a guard behind ready with his boot in case you moved. At 1 A.M. they allowed us to go to our barracks, and we were staggering from hunger and weakness. Here a pleasant surprise awaited us. Our pals had collected all the food they could find and had put it in our bunks. I assure you it tasted good.

The next morning we were brought up for trial and closely questioned as to *why* we wanted to escape. Sammy told them we wanted a change, that was all. After this we were conducted by two officers and an interpreter back to our coke ovens, and from there we were taken, one at a time, to show them where we had gotten through their lines. Blackie was taken first and he led them down a ladder and past three sentries. Sammy and I took them over the same route; and they were quite convinced that we escaped that way. That night we laughed when we saw they had an extra sentry stationed there. Already we were planning to make another attempt at getting away, and we hoped to go the same road. But instead of night duty we were put on day shift, so we had to wait another week. Before the week was out I had a narrow escape. The prisoners working in the mines were under the supervision of the large prison camp at Muenster, and once or twice a week they would send out an officer to look us over and see how we were behaving. The one chosen to look after our camp was a big burly brute, who showed his teeth and snarled like a cross dog. Even the guards were scared to death of him, and you could see them tremble and shake when he approached. No doubt they were afraid that they might lose their job if he could find any reason for reporting them. He seemed to hate the English even more than the other Germans did, and that wasn't necessary, but his chief aim in life seemed to be to catch an Englisher disobeying any of the camp rules, and as soon as he came inside our yard he would always make a bee-line for our hut. He paid no attention to the French and Russians. It was against the rules to smoke in the bunkhouse and half the time we were not allowed in the yard, so of course we broke the rule and smoked, only some one always stayed on guard and gave warning if they saw a "square-head" coming.

Well, this day I was on guard when I saw our friend coming on the run. I was standing just in the doorway, and I called out "Nix!" and the boys put their fags out of sight in a hurry. An instant later the old jay reached the door, and he stood sniffing like a dog. It didn't require any imagination to smell tobacco smoke, for the air was thick with it, but there wasn't a cigarette or pipe in sight. The old "square-head" knew that he was fooled, that some one had given them warning, and he snarled like a dog. I was standing beside the door because we were supposed to freeze whenever or wherever he appeared. He must have blamed me for warning the boys, for he whipped out his short sword, and wheeling quickly made a slash at me. That sword whizzed through the air like a bullet; and its point went an inch and a half into the frame of the door. I had ducked just in time or it would have been all off with me. I didn't wait to give him another chance, but made a bolt out of the door and over to Ruskie's hut. He went away raging, for he knew that I had slipped one over him.

While we were waiting two Russians were brought back; they had seen us go and made their escape the same way.

Jack O'Brien

They had neither map nor compass, and they were soon caught. The day they were brought back we saw them being conducted over to the coal shed; and I said, "I bet those dubs won't know any better than to show them how they escaped," and sure enough that is just what they did, so our chances in that direction were cut off, the door was securely locked and iron bars put across.

After we had been at work a little more than a week the Germans decided we needed further punishment for our attempted escape; so we were called up and the following sentences read to us by an officer who spoke a little English:

"You shall be put in a dungeon for ten days."

"You shall not see no daylight."

"You shall not have no blankets."

"You shall not take your coats."

"You shall live on bread and water."

"If you shall try to get away you shall have to die."

We couldn't keep from smiling at his attempt to write commandments. We were taken to the little prison that was in the centre of our yard. It was a tiny brick building containing only six cells; it had neither light nor ventilation, and the sanitary conditions were simply awful. It was worse than the filthiest pigpen you ever saw; and even pigs have straw to lie on, but we had nothing but the cold wet ground. The cells were more like coffins than anything else—they were just six feet by three and contained no furniture of any kind. Well, this was where we were put, and I assure you we didn't enjoy the prospect of spending ten days there. We tried to pass the time by calling to each other through the walls, but even this was forbidden, and our guard would stop it whenever he happened to overhear us. Old Blackie was very fond of good things to eat, and he always had the last of everything in sight; so Sammy and I amused ourselves by planning menus for him now that we had nothing but bread and water. We pretended that we were his servants and whenever we thought that it was getting near a mealtime we would read the menu to him. We suggested everything we had ever seen or heard of—roast turkey, frogs' legs, oysters, fruit of all kinds, etc., etc. Blackie would criticize our bill of fare, call us down for not getting something nicer, and usually ended up by ordering something entirely different. Often when we were in the midst of this nonsense, our old jailer would come knocking at our door and order us to stop talking. Blackie would say, "Boys, you could keep all your fine dinners if I could only get at that square-headed son of a gun out there. I'd make a meal out of him."

Of course none of the other prisoners were allowed to talk to us; but sometimes they would bring a book or paper and sit down with their backs against the prison wall. As long as the sentry was in sight they pretended to read, but when he was out of hearing they would tell us the camp news, and they took a special delight in telling us the good eats they had gotten in their last parcels. Of course we hadn't anything but one piece of black bread and a drink of water once a day, and we could only keep track of the days by the number of times our jailer had been in. Well, one day a chap slipped a knife blade under my door and I proceeded to make a hole in the wall. I carefully picked out the mortar until I had a hole large enough to peek through. The first one I made was too high; I didn't want to stand every time I looked out, so I plugged it up with a piece of my black bread and made another near the floor. Here I could lie down and see what was going on in the yard; and when Blackie had his imaginary breakfast he would call for the "Continental Times," and I would take the plug out of the wall and give him the morning news—what shifts were going out, who was on them, etc.

But we came near losing even this little bit of pleasure, and this is what happened: Some of the prisoners were planning an escape, and they dug a hole through the wall of their hut—the bricks were loose, ready to take out, and on the night they were to go my friend Macdonald, who was the ringleader, began to carefully remove the bricks—he took out two, and then it occurred to him that he had better take a peek out, and make sure that no one was watching, so he did; and there, only a few feet away, was a sentry, with his rifle pointed at the hole ready to blow the head off the first man who appeared. Needless to say, Mac did not go any farther; he warned the others, and they all crawled back to their bunks, and went to sleep. Next morning there was a big row made, and the guards tried to make the prisoners tell what ones were planning to escape, but no one squealed; and they were all stood "at attention" for two hours. Then a civilian was brought in with a pail of plaster, and he fixed up the hole that the prisoners had made, and with two of the officers he made the round of all the huts looking for more loose bricks. Finally he came to the prison, and one of the officers pushed the little stick he carried through the first hole I had made. This started them swearing at us, calling us English Schweinhunds and everything else they could think of. We lay there trying to keep from laughing, but at last Blackie exploded; and gee! they did rave. Finally they found the second hole, but I held my hand over it so the stick didn't come through—they could feel something soft, but had no idea what it was. Just then the officers were called away and the old civilian stopped up the top hole and moved on—no doubt the lower one is there still.

They took us out on Monday morning and we were almost

too weak to walk. The boys had a meal prepared for us, and we rested all that day. Next day they put us to work again, but instead of putting us all on the same shift they separated us. I was given night duty and the other boys were on day shift. I was feeling pretty blue the first day I went off to work alone, but was surprised and delighted to find an old pal of mine was on the same shift. This man was Macdonald, who had already made three attempts to escape, and when I met him he said, "Well, Jack, are you ready to try it again?" I said "Sure," and he said, "Well, I have everything ready and we will try and get away tonight." He had a good map and compass, so I told another prisoner to give mine to Sammie in case I got away. We knew the number of sentries and had them all located except one. It was very necessary that we should find out where he was.

Neither Mac nor I were allowed off the platform, so I asked another prisoner to let his hat blow off and then look round for a guard while he was down after it. He did this, but owing to the darkness under the platform he couldn't see anything, and he was just coming up when the gleam of a bayonet caught his eye; and here was our missing-link—with his back up against a pillar at the very spot where we had intended going over. That night at lunch hour one of the old prisoners came to us and told us to be careful, for he had heard two of the sentries planning to shoot the first one they found trying to escape. They figured that if they made an example of one, all the others would be afraid to make an attempt. We were not frightened, but they watched Mac and me so closely that we had no chance to get away. This was kept up for five nights, but on the fifth our opportunity came.

But first I must tell you what preparation we made in regard to clothes. It would not do for us to get away with only our prison garb, for it was grey, with wide red stripes down the centre of the coat, on the trouser legs, and on our caps. The only other clothes in our possession were those furnished by the Red Cross; namely, a brown sweater coat and black trousers. Now, each night before going to work, we were lined up and the officers looked us over to make sure no one had any Red Cross clothing on him. But this is how we fixed it. The black trousers had brown stripes, because the Germans insisted on our wearing stripes of some sort. When the Red Cross sent over the first parcels the Germans cut open the trouser legs and inserted red stripes. This work was so roughly done that the garments were spoiled, so the Red Cross put in brown stripes.

Now, in preparing for escape we cut this stripe out and sewed up the trousers so that they were all black. Then we cut the sweater coat up to the size and shape of our prison jacket and sewed it in. And when we lined up for examination, instead of throwing open our coats we thrust our hands in our pockets, and this opened our coats without turning back the corners. We had pulled on the prison overalls over our black trousers, so if we got away all we had to do was wear our prison jacket inside out, drop our overalls, and we were in civilian clothes. Still, each night as we lined up our hearts almost stopped beating lest they should discover our preparation. We couldn't lay in a supply of food, for just at this time there was a movement of troops at the border and the Germans were not bringing any parcels, so if we got away we must trust to what we could pick up in the fields.

But now to go back to the fifth night. As we went to lunch at twelve o'clock Mac said, "Now, Jack, we must make it tonight, for tomorrow we go on day shift." I said, "All right, Mac, I'm game; and we shall try for it just as soon as we go on duty again." We had an hour off for lunch, and as it didn't take long to eat a small piece of bread and sup a bowl of soup, we usually had a good sleep, but now we were too excited to either sleep or eat, and sat together and made our plans.

The platform on which we worked was situated in the centre of the railway yards and was as brightly lighted as the main street of a city. But this night we noticed two box-cars on a track about two hundred yards away, and Mac said, "If we can make them, we are safe." So when our hour was up and they marched us back, Mac and I were the first two up the ladder. We followed about three feet behind the first sentry until we got halfway down the platform, and while he went dreaming on his way to the end of the platform we dropped quietly to the ground. We were running when we struck, and we certainly beat the record in our two-hundred-yard dash to the box-cars, and from there to a small bush another two hundred yards away. Evidently no one noticed us, for there was not a shot fired. Once in the cover of the bush we felt safe, and we congratulated one another on having made at least a successful start. We carried our prison overalls with us, as we planned to make use of them later on.

Of course our first job was to get rid of our prison clothes, and while we were doing this we heard a great commotion in the camp. The prisoners were being lined up and counted, and we knew that we had been missed. The German rule was that if any prisoners escaped the officer in charge of the guard at that time was sent to the front lines, and this was the most dreaded of all punishments. This night a big bully was in charge, and he was hated by all the men. One of the prisoners had said early in the night, "Now, Jack, if you intend to get away, for goodness' sake go while this brute is in charge, for we want to get rid of him." We thought of this while we listened to him shouting out his orders in a voice that could be heard a mile. We knew the first thing they would do would be to put the bloodhounds on our track. They took them to our bunkhouse and let them get the scent from there. But we had a little plan to get rid of them; as soon as we heard them coming we scattered some pepper on our trail. We walked all that night, and although we heard the hounds occasionally we saw nothing of our pursuers. Morning found us on the edge of about two acres of scrub. The bushes were only about five feet high, but they were very thick and well-leaved, so we decided to lay up there for the day. Nothing happened until about four o'clock in the afternoon, when we were startled by hearing some one coming crashing through the bushes. We hugged the ground as closely as we could and hardly breathed, as the footsteps were coming nearer. The bushes were so thick that we couldn't see the person, but it sounded as though he was coming straight for us. We determined to sell our liberty dearly in case we were discovered, but to our intense relief he passed about two yards from us. We could see his feet and legs and could easily have reached out and tripped him. He was a German patrol, and he was looking for us. We watched him after he got past to make sure we wouldn't go the direction he had taken. We hadn't anything to eat that day except one piece of German black bread that each of us saved out of our rations the day before.

At 10 P.M. we started on the march again, and after about two hours' walking we came to the River Lippe. We lost no time looking for a boat, but made straight for our old bridge. It was easier getting through the wire this time, and we had no difficulty in getting across. Travelling on, we came to the little town of Haltern, but we didn't dare risk going through this time, in case some one was on the lookout for us. So we skirted around the edge, and on the way came across a few early gardens. It was early in June and nothing was very far advanced, but we found some young beets, which we ate, tops and all, also some seed potatoes. Of the latter we dug up almost the whole patch and we filled our pockets and big red handkerchiefs which each of us carried. I assure you these raw vegetables tasted as good to us then as any turkey dinner we would have at home. After our hasty lunch we started off across country. It was much rougher travelling, but we thought it was safer. Just at dawn we came to what we thought was a fair-sized bit of woods, and we decided to spend the day there. But when daylight had fully come, we found that our bush was a very small one and right at its edge was a German farmhouse. It was too late to go any farther, so we crawled along looking for a secluded spot in which to hide. Pretty soon we came to some low bushes over which a running vine had spread itself, so we crept in and lay down. Pretty soon we heard voices and the barking of a dog, and peeking out we saw an old farmer ploughing just at the edge of the bush. He was followed by two children and a dog, and as these played around we expected every minute they would land in on top of us. There was no sleep for us that day, so we lay there munching our potatoes and waiting for the darkness.

At 10 P.M. we started out, and soon we came in sight of Dulmen Camp. Once more we skirted around it, keeping as far away as possible. After a couple of hours we reached the swamp that came so near to being the death of us on our former trip. This time we went around, and though it took longer it was a vast deal more comfortable. It was too early in the night to make use of our old friend, the implement shed, but I passed it with real regret as I remembered the comfortable rest I had there. But we felt we must push on and run the risk of striking something good later in the night. We were now in the midst of a good farming district, and we decided we must lay in our rations for the following day. So, the next potato field we came to, we set to work and dug up about half of it. Potatoes were very scarce in Germany at this time. They were issued out to the farmers by the Government and could only be used for seed; and it tickled us to think how angry the old farmer would be when he discovered the

Jack O'Brien

damage done to his crop.

It was now getting on towards morning and we were very tired and weak, so the first bit of woods we came to looked good to us, and we decided to camp there for the day. On the way we picked up a tin pail and we decided to try boiling some potatoes if we got the chance. Everything seemed very quiet and it was still too early for any one to be around, so we gathered some wood and made a fire. I got some water from a nearby slough and we soon had the potatoes on; after they had been boiling for twenty minutes we tried them to see if they were nearly ready, but they seemed as hard as ever. So we waited another fifteen minutes, and still they were not soft. It was hard work waiting, for we were almost starved, but we let them boil for an hour, and Mac said we had better take them up before they got too tough to chew; so we started at them, but they were almost as tough as leather. We had nothing to eat with them but some pepper, and they had nothing to recommend them except that they were hot. After breakfast we crawled under some bushes and tried to sleep, but our nerves were too tightly strung to give us any rest.

However, we lay there all day, and nothing disturbed us. Towards evening a heavy thunderstorm came up, and it rained for two hours. Of course we were soaked to the skin, and we didn't look forward with much pleasure to our night's walk. Owing to the storm, darkness came on earlier than usual, so we got started in good time. We started out across country, and after travelling for two or three hours we came to a pasture field. We saw some cows in the distance, and Mac asked me if I could milk. I said, "It is a long time since I tried, but I would make a good stab at it for the sake of having a drink right now." Mac stayed on guard at the fence while I took our potato pail and went over to make the acquaintance of Bossy. There were three cows in the bunch, and choosing the one that looked most friendly I went up and introduced myself. I'm not sure she understood all the nice things I said to her, but her feminine vanity seemed to be pleased with the patting I gave her. At last I broached the subject of my visit, and taking "silence for consent," I took my pail and set to work; but the old lady showed her disapproval by walking away. Of course I followed, and once more resorted to flattery. When I thought I had her worked up sufficiently, I tried again for milk, but with the same result. This was repeated several times, and at last my patience was exhausted, so I hailed Mac, and when he came I urged him to continue the petting business while I tried for milk. He did this, and it worked splendidly; we got sufficient milk to give us both a good drink. It seemed to put new life into us. This was our fourth day out, and we were almost famished. After we finished our drink we thanked our old cow and started on the march again. This seemed to be our lucky night, for soon we came across a garden, and we laid in another supply of potatoes. Continuing on our way, we came to a fine road. It was bordered on each side by the most beautiful elm trees, and as it was leading in the right direction we determined to follow it. After walking about a mile we came to a farmhouse and right beside the road was a milk-stand. It held three cans of milk, and we couldn't make up our minds whether the farmer had intended them for the milkman or for us. We preferred to think the latter, so we proceeded to help ourselves.

We sat there and drank milk until we felt that we must look like "observation balloons." Then we filled our potato pail and went on. But we didn't feel much like walking and decided to lay up in the first likely-looking place that we came to. The whole country is beautifully wooded, so it was not long before we came to a nice bluff. It looked nice and quiet, and we settled ourselves for the day. We were very tired, and we both fell asleep, but I woke with a start, for I heard something coming through the bush. I wakened Mac, and we grasped our heavy walking sticks and lay still. The sound came nearer and nearer, and just when our nerves were at breaking point two bright eyes looked down at us over the edge of the little hollow we were in—it was a hedgehog. We couldn't keep from laughing at the scare it had given us. I wanted to take revenge, but Mac said, "No, let the little devil alone, it's a sign of good luck." Nothing else happened that day, and we chewed away at our raw potatoes and drank milk as we waited for darkness. When it came we started out again across country.

About 1 A.M. we came to a railroad track and after looking carefully in case there should be a sentry on guard, we crossed and came up on a carefully graded road. It was difficult travelling this night because, owing to the clouds, we had to depend entirely on our compass. We were not sure how the road ran, so while Mac got out his searchlight and endeavoured to read the compass I kept watch. If it was only getting a drink, one was always on guard. A moving figure in a field at the edge of the grade caught my attention, and at first I thought it was an animal. So it was, but of the two-legged German variety. He had seen our light, and suspecting that we were prisoners he determined to get a good shot at us. I suppose he could almost see the four hundred marks offered by the Government as a reward for a prisoner, dead or alive. He was coming in a stooping position, and the night was so dark that I wasn't sure it was a man until he raised his rifle and straightened up. Then I grabbed my chum and said, "A man, Mac," and we made a bolt for cover. The shot rang out, but he did not get us, and before our pursuer could climb the grade we were safely hidden in the bush. This was a warning that we were getting into the "danger-hole" district, for the man who shot at us was a police patrol.

Let me explain how the Holland border is guarded. It is well known that the border between Belgium and Holland is protected by a fence of *live wires*; but the Holland and German border is looked after by a wonderful system of patrols. This patrol system begins on a road two miles back from the border and running parallel with it. On this road there are three different kinds of patrols—men on horseback, on bicycles, and on foot—and instead of going singly, they were in parties of from three to ten. This is typical of the German at war and at home; he is much too cowardly to attempt anything single-handed. That's why their officers continue to send them over in massed formation; though sometimes it almost made our gunners sick the way they had to mow them down. Well, as I said, they patrolled their beats in parties; and this outside beat is well looked after. Crossing this first patrol, and leading into the border, there is a road every half-mile, and of course each road has its own special patrol—also another patrol has his beat in between these roads; while close to the border are two more lines of guards: one of these is stationary and the men are placed two hundred yards apart, and right in front of these guards, on each quarter-mile beat, walked a man, having two immense bloodhounds on leash.

Now, all this elaborate guard system was not put there for the sole purpose of catching a few escaping prisoners. But at this time the German soldiers were deserting in such large numbers, and getting over into Holland, that the Government took this method of stopping them. Now, this was what Mac and I were up against in attempting to cross the Holland border, and we realized the difficulties only too well, for Mac had learned it all by bitter experience. One stormy night, some weeks previous, he had crossed the border into Holland, only to lose his way, and stray back into Germany. He was captured by the guards and sent back to the mines. This was his third attempt as well as mine, and we knew it would go hard with us if we were caught again. So, after our brush with one of these game wardens who also acted as police patrol, we were doubly careful. We kept in the shadow of the trees and watched every step. When suddenly, right before us, shone out the whiteness of a graded road and we knew that we were in the line of the outside patrol. We crouched in the darkness at the edge of the wood and listened, but not a sound came to our ears, and in a moment or two Mac whispered "Now, Jack," and we made a dash across, when to our utter amazement three figures sprang up right in front of us and we found ourselves looking into three rifle barrels. A gruff German voice called, "Halt! Who goes there?" and we threw up our hands and grunted a reply. Immediately the guns were lowered and the men came toward us, but instead of finding two helpless prisoners, they were met by good hard blows delivered in true British fashion. We had taken them completely by surprise, and in a few minutes we were able to break through. We didn't wait to see what condition they were in, but made the best time possible to a place of safety. We heard one of them blow his whistle, just after we got away, and a couple of shots were fired, but if reinforcements came we did not see them. We kept on going until we thought we were safe from pursuit, and we began looking for a place in which to lay up for the day. This was our seventh day without food excepting raw vegetables, and our strength was almost exhausted.

This encounter with the patrols had used us up pretty badly owing to our weakened condition, and we knew that the supreme test was still ahead. Presently, right in the centre of the bush, we came to a place where the slough grass was very long and thick, and we decided to risk spending the day there. We were now in the centre of the patrol district, and there was no *safe* place; but we hoped to be fortunate enough not to be too close to the beat of the nearest patrol. We pulled a quantity of long grass and buried ourselves in it.

Although very tired, sleep was out of the question, and we lay there planning how we could get through the last two lines of guards.

About 8 A.M. we were alarmed by the noise of some one crashing through the bushes, and our hearts beat like hammers as we listened to the sound growing nearer. Of course we were sure it was a patrol, and we began to fear our little game was up. We lay there scarcely breathing, and all at once voices reached us, and Mac whispered to me, "Gee! they must have women in this patrol." We peered through the grassy cover, and there, coming straight towards us, were two young German girls. The wooden shoes they wore accounted for the great racket they made, but I assure you we felt very much relieved, though our danger was still very great, for they could give the alarm, and we did not know who might be near.

A short distance from us they took off their coats, and we saw they had come to work. All through this part of the woods were scattered bundles of small sticks for firewood, and the girls' job was to collect these and carry them to a road some three hundred yards distant. The young ladies kept up a continual chatter, and perhaps it was this that kept them from discovering our hiding-place, for they came within two or three yards of us. At twelve o'clock they started home, and as soon as they were out of sight we got up and stretched ourselves. It was so good to move after lying still for four hours. However, we didn't dare stay up very long, and we were "tucked in" once more when the girls got back. This time there were three, and they worked away until about four o'clock. We had to lie like mice, and we were in constant terror lest one of us should sneeze or cough. Just about four we heard one girl say "Fertig" (or "finished"), and the three went out and sat on the side of the wood to continue their chat. We felt very much relieved and were congratulating ourselves on another escape when we heard a man's voice, and looking out of our hiding-place we saw an old man in conversation with the girls. He had evidently counted the bundles and was insisting that there were still some left in the bush. They argued for quite a while, and then to please the old man the girls came back. But it was evident they felt sore over having to come, for instead of searching for wood, they walked right through the bush and out to the road on the other side. There they sat down and after awhile moved on home, or at any rate out of sight. We were glad to be able to move again and to be relieved of our uninvited company. As soon as we were sure they were not coming back we got up and moved around to get the ache out of our bones. We also had some preparations to make for our final effort that night. As I mentioned before, we had carried our prison overalls with us, and now we were to put them to use. Our only chance of getting over the border lay in our being able to move so quietly that the sentry could not hear us. So we started to make moccasins out of our discarded overalls. We had neither scissors, needles, nor thread, but our experience had taught us that in all circumstances we must make *what we did have* serve our purpose. Our jackknife cut out our moccasins, and it also made a small stick into an implement that could punch holes, while some pieces of cord that we happened to have did fine in place of thread. It took quite a while to get our moccasins made, working with poor tools, and they were fancy-looking articles when we at last had them finished. The red trimming was very fetching, but we thought it quite appropriate, for there is always a lot of *red tape* necessary in getting out of a country that is *At War*. It was almost dark when we had our moccasins finished, so we put them on and made ready for our start. Our boots were securely fastened to our belts, and we took a final look at our map. We were almost famished, but two raw potatoes was all that remained in "the larder." However, we disposed of these, and just at 11 o'clock we started out.

The direction to the border was straight west, and we figured it must be a mile and a half to the nearest point. But we had to keep under cover as much as possible, so we couldn't tell just when we might be near it. We crossed the wood at the side of our bush, and a few minutes' walk brought us in sight of a small pasture field in which there were three or four cows. The sight of these brought to our minds the dandy drink of milk we had two nights before, and though we took an awful risk, going out into the open, we thought it worth while. Once more Mac stood on guard, and I crawled out to where the cows were grazing. I tried them, one after another, but not a drop of milk could I get. They had evidently been milked a short time previous. I made the trip back in safety, and we started out, not knowing what minute we might happen on a sentry's beat, which made our going exceedingly slow.

About 12.30 we came to the edge of a swamp, and here and there all through it we saw dark objects that looked like men. We lay in the long grass and watched to see if we could notice any movement. Sometimes we thought there was, and then again we were sure they were stationary. However, we had to pass them, so we crawled carefully forward, and made our way close to where one of these objects was standing, and when we thought we were near enough we raised up and took a look. It was a stack of peat piled to just about the size of a man. We had a good laugh, and I assure you we felt very much relieved. We made our way safely across the swamp and had just reached the other side when we heard the hounds. We listened, and noted that the sound came from across the swamp, just the direction we had come. Mac said, "Jack, they are on our track; we had better put out some pepper;" so we sprinkled it on our tracks and, crouching as low as possible, moved along. The sound was getting nearer, and suddenly, to our right, we heard a sentry call "Halt!" But instead of stopping we ran for all we were able. We heard the sentry call three times, and then a shot rang out. There was no attempt at concealment now, we were running for our lives, or what was dearer still—our *liberty*. There was a grove of trees just ahead, and we knew that we still had a chance if we could reach that. One more spurt and we were there, and had thrown ourselves down with our faces toward the open country we had just left. We were pretty well out of breath, but we dared not stay longer than was necessary to get our wind, so we pushed on, for we were anxious to get across the border in the darkest part of the night. We stole along like ghosts, for we did not know what moment we might run up against the border guards. We decided that the shot we had heard on our right had come from a passing patrol.

We kept on until 4 A.M., and as it was getting a little bit light we saw in the distance what looked like a small town. We were much astonished, because if we read our map aright the only town on our route should have been passed the night before. We lay up in a field and talked it over, but we couldn't locate ourselves. It wouldn't do for us to lay up for a day so near a town, so we must either turn back or hasten on. At last I said, "Let's flip a coin and see which we will do— heads, we go on; tails, we turn back." We did this, and it turned out "heads," so on we went. I forgot to say between us and the town was a canal, and we couldn't find a bridge. This canal was another puzzling feature. Well, we swam it, and came out very wet, cold, and tired. We passed within half a mile of the town and finally struck the main road on the other side. It was now daylight, and we had to be on the lookout for people every instant. Finally we saw a signpost just ahead, and we thought that would surely solve our problem. But when we came to it we found the lettering had become almost obliterated. One town that the hand pointed to we figured out as "Neda," but the one we had just passed could not be made out. Finally, with Mac's help, I climbed up to the top of the pole, and from there I made out a few of the letters. Comparing these with an address I had found on a piece of wrapping paper earlier in the morning, I made out the name as "Haakshergen." However, our map didn't show either of these towns, so we were just as much at sea as ever.

Then it occurred to us that the border troops must be stationed in either one of these towns, and there would surely be some of them passing on this road; so we determined to hide in the ditch close by and watch for them. We came to a place where there were some bushes growing at the side of the ditch and we hid in these. Finally we saw two mounted men coming, but they passed so quickly that we couldn't see much except that they wore grey uniforms. We waited a little longer, and along came two soldiers on foot. One of these was evidently sick or wounded, for just as they came opposite us he begged to be allowed to sit down. They talked for a minute or two and then moved on, but we had a good look at them. They wore exactly the same uniform as the German excepting that their hats were different. Instead of a "pill-box" they had a cap with a square top. All at once I remembered having seen some pictures of Holland soldiers in the *Daily Mirror* (an English paper), and I said, "By golly, I believe they are Hollanders," but Mac said, "No; if they were, they wouldn't be dressed like Germans." One thing we decided on, and that was that we must find a safer place than the one we were in; so when there was no one in sight we made our way to a nearby wheat field. We lay there discussing the situation, and just at 9 o'clock we heard the whistle of a train. We could hardly believe our ears, and we crawled to the edge of the field to see in which direction it was going. We found it running right into the town we had passed, and now we were more muddled than ever, for the German town that we thought was on the border hadn't a railroad nearer than fifteen kilometers. We made our way back into the field, took out our map, and tried to solve the problem.

At last we got desperate; we couldn't go on at night unless we found out where we were, so we thought we would take a chance on going farther down the road. We hadn't gone far when we saw a man in the distance, and we slipped into some bushes until he had passed. Going on farther we saw there was a man coming on a bicycle. We ducked and hid, and as he got nearer we could see that he had a gun strapped on his shoulders. We were afraid he had seen us and we were sure there would be some fun, but fortunately he too passed. When everything was quiet we started out again, and presently we spied an old man working on the road. He had only a wheelbarrow and shovel, so we decided to risk asking him what country we were in. When we came up we bid him the time of day, and, in the best German we could muster, asked, "Which is this, Germany or Holland?" The old man looked at us, smiled, and said "*This is Holland.*" It sounded too good to be true, and for an instant we could only stare at him and each other, then the realization came that we were *FREE* and we laughed and hugged one another in our joy. The old man watched us with a sympathetic smile, for though he could not understand all that we were saying he knew that we were escaped prisoners. We must have been a rough-looking pair. We had travelled a hundred miles at night over all kinds of country, and had been eight days without any cooked food. Our faces were covered with hair, and our clothes were ragged and dirty. I weighed only 125 pounds, and the long period of anxiety and mental strain, had aged me at least ten years. Mac was just as bad, and we must have looked more like a couple of jail-birds than anything else.

Well, finally we sobered down sufficiently to ask the man

how far it was to the nearest town. He told us it was about five miles to the little town of "Neda"; but before we started he asked us if we were hungry. We looked at each other and smiled—and the old man understood—he insisted on our taking all of his lunch, even the bottle of tea that he carried—and I assure you no food ever tasted better. We felt like new men after getting something to eat, and we shall not soon forget the old Hollander's kindness to us. It was with light hearts that we finally said "Good-bye" to our new friend and started on our way to "Neda."

The world looked very different to what it had a few hours before, and we were so busy talking about our experiences that we scarcely noticed a man passing by us on a bicycle. He must have heard a scrap of the conversation, for he turned and looked, and then jumped off his wheel and came toward us. He said, "Are you Englishmen?" We said, "No, not exactly; we are Canadians." "Oh," he said, "Canadians. I am a Hollander myself, but I was educated in England; you must be escaped prisoners." We replied, "Oh, we are not telling *what* we are." He said, "You needn't be afraid, for my sympathy is all with the Allies." So we told him everything, and he walked with us until we got almost to Neda. Then he mounted his wheel and rode into town, telling every one in sight that we were coming. So when we arrived the streets were lined with people; men, women, and children turned out to welcome us. They finally conducted us to a store where the proprietor spoke English. We sat and chatted for a few minutes, and then his wife came out with a lunch. She brought bread and butter, cake and tea, and I leave you to imagine how good it tasted.

But our friend on the wheel had left us at the store, and had reported our coming to the police headquarters. So while we were at our lunch the chief of police and an attendant arrived and asked us to go with them. This didn't look good to us—it seemed too much like what we had been getting for the past year. I said, "By golly!! Mac, I don't like this." He said, "Neither do I, but I guess we have to go," so we went along; but instead of landing in the police station, the chief took us to his own house. Here we were made to understand we were *guests*; and we were given water, soap, clean towels, and fresh shirts to replace the ones that were torn to pieces. After we got cleaned up we felt like new men, and our host took us out where a table was set under the trees and we had our first properly served meal since leaving England—a year and nine months.

Of course we were not given a regular dinner—our friends were too wise for that—heavy food would have killed us. All we had was bread and butter, cake, and strawberries with cream; but oh, they were scrummy. The next thing we needed was sleep, and our host wished to put us to bed in the house. But we felt much too dirty to get into his clean beds, and we made him understand we much preferred going into the hayloft. So he brought us some blankets, and we turned in. We slept for fourteen hours without waking; that's how badly we needed it. We wakened at 2 A.M., and at first we didn't know where we were. But after we got our bearings we went to sleep again and didn't wake until nine in the morning. Then we got up and had another light meal. We lay around and rested all that day, but as their English was as limited as our Dutch, conversation lagged. That night we had our first taste of meat since entering Germany—and maybe we didn't enjoy it!

Early next morning we took the train for Rotterdam, the chief sending an escort with us. Once there, we were taken to the British consul, and after proving our identity we were given clothes, money, and a passport for England. It was ten days before we got a boat out of Rotterdam, and during that time we received nothing but kindness from the people we met.

Finally we secured passage on a boat, and on the *first day of July* we landed in England.

Jack O'Brien

"MY COMRADES, AND WHAT BECAME OF THEM, AS TOLD TO ME IN LETTERS, BY MY OLD CHUM BOB GODDARD."

DEAR JACK:

Well, you certainly had a pretty tough time in Germany, and I don't envy your experience. And now you want to hear what we did after you were taken prisoner, and what became of the bunch that you and I knew so well. It's not pleasant to recall the things that happened, Jack, but I'll do my best. Let me see; the Battle of St. Eloi was the last scrap you took part in. Well, after that things cooled down a bit, but we still took our turn in the trenches on that part of the line. No. 10 Platoon was still intact. We missed poor old Woodrow, and his chum Fred went around looking like a ghost. The latter had never gotten over his experience in No Man's Land, his eyes were sunken in his head, and he was nothing but a wreck. One night, when we were in reserves in Dickiebush, a few of us were talking and saying how lucky our little bunch had been, when at that minute an order came in sending us out on a working party. Fritz had gotten busy and blown down a section of our front lines, and the boys holding this spot had no protection, so we were being sent up to repair the damage. I guess Fritz was sore, for our Stokes light trench mortars and heavies had been pounding the German trenches all day long. Well, we were told off in small parties to carry up sandbags, corrugated iron, picks and shovels, to repair the line.

Our little bunch consisted of Tommy, Bink, Scottie, Bob Richardson, Newell, McMurchie, and one or two others whom you do not know. "Flare-pistol Bill" was in charge, of course; and just our luck, we had to carry the corrugated iron (and damned awkward stuff it is), it's too wide to carry through the trenches, so we had to go overland—and I tell you, the machine gun fire was wicked. The boys holding the trenches had a lot of casualties. Well, we got our loads and started off in and out of shell holes. Tommy fell into a hole that was full of water and got soaked; and Chappie, with his poor eyesight, if he fell once, he fell at least a dozen times. We went along cursing our hard luck, and making the best time we could, for the bullets were flying mighty thick. Flares were going up every few minutes, and every time one went up we would "freeze" till it went out again. At last we got quite close to the front line, and when Fritz sent up a flare it would fall right behind us. They couldn't help seeing us, for we made a lovely target with those big slabs of corrugated iron on our heads. The machine guns just ripped lead at us, and we were hurrying to get to the trench, when young Blair got it through the thigh. He started to yell at the top of his voice; and Scottie, who happened to be next in line, cussed him roundly for the noise he was making. We would likely have been all killed if he hadn't shut up. Well, they bound him up and carried him out, and the rest of us went on.

We hadn't gone fifty feet when Scottie went down with a crash, just in front of me. I crawled up to him, and he was badly hit—the blood was pouring from his mouth, and he mumbled "Stretcher bearer." Flare-pistol Bill went on to the trench to hunt up one, and I crawled back to see if I could find the one who had come up with us. Before I got back with Bob the stretcher bearer from the trench had fixed Scottie up as well as he could. Poor Scottie! his jaw was shattered. Bink insisted on carrying Scottie out on his shoulders, and they started. But before going halfway Bink played out, and when Scottie saw that Bink was all in he got down and walked to the dressing-station. Say, that boy was sure game. By the way, he's in Blighty now. Well, the rest of us got through safely, we fixed up our trench and managed to get back to our supports. A few nights later we made another trip to the front lines, and this was disastrous for No. 10. First of all, Tucker got shot in the face while on a wiring party; then Jack Branch was on a working party behind the trench when Fritzie started shelling, and he got a shrapnel bullet through his arm. We bound him up, and he was in great pain, but he smiled all the time. As he went out, he said, "I'll give your love to all the girls at Shorncliffe." I thought, "Well, isn't this a hell of a war, when a man can be pleased over getting a bloomin' big hole through his arm?"

Later that same night Tommy Gammon was on sentry go, and I was sleeping in the dugout behind him, when Corporal Banks came in and woke me. He said, "Do you want to see Tommy? He's hit." Gee, I jumped up in a hurry and ran down the trench to where Tommy was; but I breathed freely when I saw that it was only a hole through his arm—I was afraid he had got it bad. "How did you get it, Tommy?" I said. He said, "Oh, you know the sandbags we rolled out of the way to fire through last night?—well, I thought some one might be walking past and get a bullet through his bean, as a fellow had farther down the trench, so I put up my arm to roll the bag into place, and *bingo*! Fritzie was right on the job." I wrote to Tommy's mother that night and told her that I thought Tommy had a Blighty, and she came all the way out from Canada to see him. But he didn't get farther than our base hospital, and he was back to the trenches again in six months, so his mother did not see him after all.

Well, after Tommy left us, we were sent back to rest billets, and it was then that the Battle of Hooge started. We could bear the guns roaring and at night the whole sky on our left was lit up. The roads were jammed with machine guns, marching troops, cyclists, and cavalry—while coming from the scene of battle was a constant stream of ambulances. Tales of what was going on came leaking through and we fully expected to be sent up. But we couldn't move without orders, and we thought we might just as well enjoy ourselves, so we got up an open-air concert. It certainly was a dandy, and we had no end of a time. A lot of the old boys took part; and then some one got up and gave us a parody on "The Sunshine of Your Smile." It goes like this:

"Oh, Fritzie that hands those Blighties out so free,
Just send a nice sweet cushy one to me—
One that will strike me just below the knee.
Six months in Blighty—oh, how sweet 'twould be!

"Send me a shell with pellets nice and round;
Scatter them, all but one, upon the ground;
Send me that one, but let it come a mile,
And I will give you the sunshine of my smile."

This met with great applause, and we sang it till we all learned the words. The concert was scarcely over when our officers told us that word had come for us to be ready to move at a moment's notice. After talking to some of our wounded boys that had come back from the fighting, we began to realize that something very serious was happening. They told us that whole battalions of Canadians had been wiped out by shell fire. Fritzie had just blown everything to pieces before he advanced, just the same as he did at St. Eloi. We realized that our time on rest was likely to be cut short; so we got busy and spent all our money—and sure enough, next day the order came for us to move, and away we went along the road to V—just behind Ypres. We reached there safely and some of our officers and N. C. O.'s went on up to the lines to see what kind of a place we were going into. They found that we would be on the left flank of the attack, and although the Germans had blown most of the front line to pieces, they had not attempted to advance here. That night two companies, A and B, were sent on ahead of the rest of us, and they went as near the lines as they could in motor-buses, then they took over what was left of the front lines, consisting mostly of shell holes. The rest of us were marched through Ypres, and we found it a mass of ruins. It was here that we saw the affects of war—dirty, horrible, stinking war. Hundreds of people were buried when Ypres was bombarded, and the stench of the place was unbearable. We followed the railroad for a piece and we passed some shell holes made by the "Fat Berthas" used by the Germans at the beginning of the war. You could bury an ordinary-sized house in any one of these holes. Dead horses were lying everywhere, showing that the road we were on had been shelled earlier in the evening. We didn't know what minute they would open up again, so we hurried over every crossroad. Fritzie had a mania for shelling crossing roads, and those in the Ypres salient are all named appropriately. Here are a few: "Shrapnel Corner," "Hellfire Corner," "Hell Blast Corner." We were marching in single file by this time, and every man carried a sandbag, bomb, rifle and bayonet, rations and a bottle of water. Some load, eh? Judging from the flares going up all around us, we seemed to be going into a pocket. On our right, the machine guns were going all the time, and they sounded like a thousand riveting machines, only instead of construction their noise meant destruction. Pretty soon we came to a big barrier of sandbags known as "China Wall," and here dead men were lying everywhere, and we couldn't help stumbling over them on our way in. At last we came to the communicating trench, and just as we reached it Fritzie sent a salvo of shells across—one or two of the boys caught it—the rest of us kept on our way. We followed the trench, scrambling over parts that were blown in, and stumbling over the dead that were lying everywhere. Finally we came to the trench that we were going to take over, and we relieved what was left of the Royal Canadian Rifles. They were an awful sight, dirty and bloodstained—many were shaking as though with a palsy—their nerves literally torn to pieces by the shell fire. But they had no word of complaint. "All right, boys, it's quiet. All's over now," was their greeting, but what they said didn't sound exactly true, for we had not been in five minutes, when with a roar all of Fritzie's guns opened up once more. Bullets swept over us like hail; it was hell let loose. The officer in charge was killed almost at once, and Major Q—took over the command. I sat in a bay with Sammy, Emerson, and Sergeant-Major Banks; the other boys were farther along the trench. I had never seen anything like what we were getting; machine guns were enfilading our trench—just at my feet was an old empty water can, and the bullets going in sounded as though some one was playing a drum. They couldn't hit me, because I was behind a traverse, or jog in the trench. After a while it quieted down a little, but it didn't entirely stop, and next morning, just at dawn, it started again, and I hope that I shall never be called on to go through what I did that day. But if I lived to be a hundred I could never forget it. Our trench was literally blown to pieces, and we couldn't do a thing but sit there and curse our gunners for not firing back—no doubt they were doing all they could, but the terrific noise of bursting shells all around us drowned the sound of our own artillery, and we fancied that we were not being supported. Wounded men were crawling along the trench looking for a spot that would offer comparative safety, and the rest of us were sitting in a daze. I was suffering for a drink, and I had no water. I had started to make some tea, but a shell knocked a big chunk of dirt into the trench and it upset my canteen. I wouldn't ask any of the boys for water, for every one needed all they had, and we are supposed to look after our own. Finally I got desperate, for the smoke and gas from the bursting shells parches the throat, and I made a search through a dead man's pack. It wasn't pleasant work, but I found a tin of milk, and it was worth a million dollars to me then. I had just gotten my drink, when, all at once, the earth under my feet began to heave and I was thrown on my face. I scrambled up again, but the earth was rocking like a ship at sea. Finally it stopped, and we looked over to the front lines which were held by A and B companies, but all we could see was smoke, black smoke right up to the sky, and then we realized what had happened. Our front lines had been blown up with mines, and now all the artillery that had been playing on our front lines was lifted on to us, and our hell became worse than ever. Then the Germans came and we had our hands full. A machine gun battery in a strong point just ahead held out, and a trench mortar on our left supported us, and our few lads did the rest. We were using the Ross rifle, and we fired it till it jammed; then we grabbed some Lee-Enfields that had been left behind by the E. C. R.'s. Fritzie seemed doped, and he came forward carrying full kit and trench mats. They were evidently surprised to find any one alive, for when we began to fire they stared around stupidly. Then our fire caught him, and as he attempted to get through the gap in our front lines the portion of line that had not been mined swept him with their machine guns. All the time our boys were just being wiped out with shell fire. Little Henry Wright was hit in the knee and started to crawl out over the back of the trench. I grabbed him and brought him back and stuck him into a hole out of the way of flying splinters. "You won't leave me, will you, if you have to go back?" he cried. "Not on your life," said I. "But don't be afraid—Fritzie is not going to chase us out of here." Just then somebody came along and said that the Germans had broken through on our right. I looked at Sammy and said, "This back to back stuff isn't all it's cracked up to be, is it?" Sammy grinned and we went on firing, and an officer that came along told us that the report we heard was not true—our line still held.

Just then poor old Baldy was blown to pieces by a shell; he had thrown up his bomb-proof job and had come back to the battalion. Chappie was struck by a piece of that same shell, and he got it right through the lung. Oh, how he did suffer! We couldn't take him back to the dressing-station on account of the terrific shell fire, and he lay in a sheltered part of the trench slowly bleeding to death. We took turns in going to see him. "Tell my little girl that I died fighting," he said to Bink. His chum, Marriot, came rushing along—"Oh, deah boy, I'm so sorry you are hit—cheer up, old chap." He, like the rest of us, didn't know what to say. But old Chappie didn't "go west" after all. He was ill for a long time, but was finally invalided home to Canada.

While we were worrying over old Chappie a call came for volunteers to dig out some men that had been buried. McLeod and I grabbed shovels, and away we went in the direction pointed out. There was smoke everywhere and shells were continually coming. We went down the trench for quite a distance, and, turning a corner, what a sight met our eyes! There, sitting around on the firing-step of a bay, were nine of our boys, dead. The shell must have burst just above them, for they were full of holes, and their clothes were on fire. I turned to Mac: "Nothing for us to do here, old boy," and we started back. Just then I stumbled over something, and looking down, I saw that it was a body almost entirely buried in the dirt and wire netting. I scraped away some of the dirt and found that the man still breathed, so I got busy and tried to get him out. He was covered with the wire that is used to keep our trenches from caving in, and it was an awful job getting the wire and dirt off. We dug with our shovels, and tore at the wire until finally we got him

Jack O'Brien

extricated. We couldn't see a wound, but we thought it might be concussion, but when we lifted him up there was a hole in his back that I could put my fist in. Poor fellow, I saw that it was no use, but I threw some water in his face, and he opened his eyes, and tried to speak, and then quietly "went west." I went back to the boys feeling mighty blue, and their only greeting was, "Where in hell have you been? Don't you know your place is here?" but I just cursed back, and explained.

The Germans had stopped coming over by this time, but they still held portions of our front line. Out of the five hundred men who took over our portion of the front trenches, only one or two came out, and this is what they told us. They had been shelled for hours and their casualties were very heavy, as their only protection was shell holes. Then Fritzie started to come over, but they gathered in a bunch and bombed him back, and then the mines went up and that finished them. When Fritzie came over the few that were left were half buried and dazed, and had lost their rifles, so they were taken prisoners.

In the second line there were about a hundred of us left. Spud Murphy, our officer, fought till his arm was disabled, but we continued to hold the trench. Bink and Sammy took a bunch of bombers and went up to the advance post; and that left our numbers still smaller. Just then Sergeant Faulkener came in from the strong point wounded in the shoulder. He had tried to keep it a secret, but loss of blood made him so weak that he had to give up. I spoke to him, and he said, "Ain't this hell? I get hit every little scrap I get into." He had been wounded down at Kemmil when Fritzie blew up the trenches there. "Honest John" we used to call him, and he was a good old scout.

The shell fire was still on just as bad as ever. Bob

Richardson, our stretcher bearer, was working like a hero, the wounded lying all around him, and often the poor fellows were hit again before he got through binding them up. A boy went past me with a bandage on his head. I said, "Hello, Jack, got a Blighty?" He said, "No, I'm afraid it's not bad enough for that." Poor fellow, he was shot through the eyes, and he didn't know that he would never see again.

That afternoon, in response to an urgent request for help, a company of men from the 29th came in. Towards evening the shelling died down a bit, and the wounded that could walk went out. Carrying parties arrived, and took out those who were badly wounded. Chappie was one of the first to go. That night the Sergeant came along and said, "Goddard and Wilson, go out on listening-post." We looked at the spot where he wanted us to go. Fritzie was landing shells there about one a minute, and there was absolutely no protection. I said "Say, Sergeant, that's suicide!" "I know," said he, "but I have orders to put a post there." I said, "All right, but if I get killed I'll come back and haunt you." Well, over the top we went and we got to the place he had pointed out; we had barely lain down in a shell hole when *whiz-bang*! a shell landed just in front of us. It covered us with dirt, and we had hardly gotten the dust out of our eyes when *whiz-bang*! another landed just behind us. "Now," thinks I, "if one comes between those two, our name is mud." It wasn't more than a minute when we heard another coming, and this one landed in the part of the trench we had just left. Shrieks and groans went up, and Wilson and I lay there shaking like leaves. Just then, the Sergeant came out and told us to go back into the trench, and you bet we were glad to do it. We found that the last shell had killed three and wounded six, and no doubt we would have gotten one had we stayed. It's funny how things happen—our Sergeant-Major was badly wounded, and I helped to carry him to a place of comparative safety, but the poor fellow died after his wounds were dressed. We buried

Jack O'Brien

the dead as best we could, and then we hung on for two days more. We had no water and scarcely any food, and we suffered terribly, especially from thirst. Our ration parties were all killed trying to get food to us. Bink and some of the boys on the outpost were relieved first, and they brought us water. Poor lads, they had been sitting on an old culvert with water up to their waists. The only sleep we got all this time was during the day when we lay in the mud at the bottom of the trench. We were relieved on the third night, and oh, what joy when the 29th came in and took over the trench! We were "all in," and we staggered back to Ypres throwing away everything we carried except our rifles. When we got to Ypres, we found that we had to go back to where we had started from, so we struggled on. On the way we met a bunch of Lancashire men. "What do you belong to?" they asked us as they passed. "We are all that is left of a Canadian battalion," we replied. "Gorblimey, it's bleedin' orful," said they. Just as day was breaking we hit camp. The Quarter-master gave us a drink of rum, and the cooks had a feed ready, and we got our blankets and turned in. We slept till the afternoon, and then we had to answer a muster call. Two hundred and seventy-two was all that was left of what, three days before, had been a battalion one thousand strong. Tears rolled down our old Colonel's face as he looked at us. "My boys! my boys!" was all he could say. We were only out twenty-four hours, and during that time we read our mail, wrote a few letters, and opened our parcels. There were parcels everywhere, many of them belonging to boys who had been either killed or wounded, and these were distri-buted among those that remained. We were dead-tired and we were hoping for a good long rest, when in marched a big bunch of reinforcements, and shortly after we received orders to pack up and be ready to move that night. It was raining when we started out, and oh! we did feel rotten to have to go back to that hell-hole again. But the new fellows didn't know what it was like, and we laughed and joked with them. Bob Tait and I were carrying No. 10's rations; and we were "connecting file"—that is, we kept in sight of the platoon behind. It was raining so hard that we were soon soaked to the skin, and we were glad when they stopped at Ypres that night. Bob and I missed the platoon in front, they went into some dugout, so we went in with the rear platoon. We were billeted in what had been an old wine cellar. The house which had been there before the war was blown down, and from the outside it looked like nothing but a pile of bricks. Bob and I were in a little place by ourselves; we knew that it was useless to try and find our own platoon in the dark. We had nothing but a stone slab to sleep on, and it didn't look very inviting to stretch out there in our wet clothes. I was just preparing to lie down when Bob said, "Wait a minute, see what I found," and he held up a bottle of rum. Gee, I could have kissed him!—we had a good drink, and maybe we weren't glad that we carried the rations that night. We had a fine sleep in spite of the artillery thundering overhead. Every now and then a heavy German shell would land right on top of our sleeping-place, but it couldn't break through. The concussion would put out the candles, that was all. That night, the First Division of Canadians and some British troops made their big counter-attack; and took back all the ground that the Germans had taken in the previous nine or ten days.

Bob and I woke up next morning and had our breakfast, and after awhile we wandered out around town. Some German prisoners were coming down the road, and we stopped and spoke to them. One who could speak a little English said, "Too much shell." They were very hungry; one of them spotted a piece of biscuit beside the road. He grabbed it up and ate it like a dog. All at once we heard a shout, and turning we spied Bink and Charlie Pound. When they got up to us they said, "Where the devil have you fellows been? We want our rations." They seemed quite peeved and they hadn't worried a bit about losing us. It was not having their rations that bothered them.

Well, that night we went back to the same trenches that we had left just three nights before, only this time we marched on the Ypres-Menin road. This is the worst road in the salient; the Germans sweep it with their machine guns every night, and it sure is wicked. Of course Rust had been over it months before and knew all about it. He told us that the bullets come about a foot from the ground, and if a fellow gets one in the leg, he will get hit again before he can crawl away. We were nicely started down the road when all at once the machine guns started to crackle. I took one jump and landed, rifle and all, in a ditch full of water. Most of the boys came with me, but I couldn't help laughing at some of the reinforcements. They took refuge behind trees, just as if a little tree would stop a machine gun bullet. Of course we told them, but not till one or two of their number got hit did they realize their danger. The Germans were shelling the trenches that we were going into, and now and again they would send over some high-explosive shells and sweep our road with shrapnel, so we had a few more casualties.

Well, at last we reached the trenches, and McMurchie and I stopped to help a fellow that was hit. By the time we got in our boys had relieved the 29th, who had been holding it ever since we left. Well, just as Mac and I jumped into the trench, we heard some one say to our Sergeant, "The officer wants you to send a couple of men for the bombing-post on the road; the two that were holding it have just been killed." Donnslau turned around and spied us making tracks up the trench. "Goddard and McMurchie, you will take charge of the bombing-post at the end of the trench: Sergeant Oldershaw will show you where it is." Mac was ticked to death, and I followed him looking as happy as I could—but, say, I wasn't feeling a bit heroic. We went on the post and

Fritzie shelled us there for two days, and it sure was a marvel that we didn't get hit. I remember, we were lying on the cobblestones in the middle of the road—the idea being to stop any Germans that might be sneaking down that way. Sometimes when things got too hot the Sergeant would call us into the trench and let us stay there for awhile. While in the trench we would go around whistling; and he was always cooking up tea or something. We always burned candles for this, and when our supply ran out he went and borrowed from the officers. Nothing seemed to bother him, and he would watch the shells bursting overhead—big black shrapnel and "woolly bears." When the latter burst they make a noise like a ton of bricks being dumped, and Mac would watch them with a smile—once when we were sitting in the mud, and I suppose I was looking about as cheerful as a dying duck in a thunderstorm, Mac remarked, "In spite of orl 'is trials and privations, the British Tommy remyns as cheerful as ever." He brought it out just like a Cockney, and I just had to smile. Shortly after this along came "Fat." He and Bink had been up at the culvert, and they were supposed to be on their way out, but poor old Fat was so stiff with the cold that he couldn't walk. We offered to fetch him a snort of rum, but he said he wouldn't take it. I suppose he had promised some darn girl back home, and he would die rather than break his word. Well, we gave him some hot tea, took off his socks and rubbed his feet; and I got him a pair of my dry socks. After awhile we coaxed him to eat a little, and we joked with him, till at last he gave a bit of a smile—and soon we heard his familiar "Tee he, tee he!"—he had the funniest laugh I ever heard. Well, he stayed with us till we were relieved.

A funny thing happened up the trench that same day. Marriot and some of the other boys were sitting in one of the bays of the trench cooking some Maconachie rations, when *bang!* right through the parapet came a shell. It went between

Marriot and the next chap, and the shock must have been awful. Marriot rushed into the next bay, and meeting our Sergeant he spluttered, "Oh say, old chap, ain't I a lucky devil? All those fellows in the next bay are blown to hell, and I escaped." The Sergeant rushed around to find the bay empty except for the shell which hadn't exploded, but was reposing quietly in the bottom of the trench and Marriot had been too excited to notice. Maybe he didn't get chipped about it afterwards. That night we were relieved by the Coldstream Guards; and say, Jack, they are soldiers! They came in like clockwork, every man knew his place, and exactly where to go. They fixed bayonets on entering the trench and there was no confusion. They had taken over the trench almost before we knew it.

How glad we were to be relieved no one knows but those who were there. We were not sorry to see the last of Hooge. They gave us about a week's rest and then we went back to our old trenches at—. It was quiet there, and for awhile we had it pretty easy. Just after taking over these trenches we were treated to a great sight. Our aeroplanes made a general attack all along the British front from the coast to the Somme, and they burned all the German observation balloons. We stood and watched them come down in flames, and it was great. Mind you it meant a lot to us; while they were watching us there couldn't be a stir behind our lines but we would be treated to a salvo of shells. In fact, we had orders not to move around in the daytime. But after the balloons were gone we could go about with comparative freedom. Even one man would attract the attention of these German eyes. Our old boy, Charlie Pound, was a runner or dispatch carrier between the front line and Headquarters, and he often came up to see us when we were in the line. One day he said, "There's a fat Fritzie in that balloon that I'd like to get my hands on; he must have a grudge against me, for he shells me every time I go down the communication trench."

So Charlie was tickled to death when that particular balloon was brought down.

Well, Jack, our next trip in was at Hill 60, and it was a warm spot—not artillery fire this time, but trench mortars. Every morning Fritzie would send us "sausages" for breakfast; they came at the rate of one a minute. It wasn't that they caused so many casualties, but they made so much work. Every day Fritzie would blow up our front line and we would have to build it up again each night under machine gun fire. We took it in turns, half of us would be on working parties and the other half on outpost duty. One night several of us were down in a cutting on a bombing-post. The cutting had once been the Ypres Commines railway and it ran across the German lines as well as through ours. We had strong posts there to keep the Fritzies back in case they took a notion to come over. In the daytime it was exposed to rifle fire. We were sitting there this night when our Corporal came running in and said, "Hurry back to the trench, there's a show going to start." He had scarcely finished speaking when the trench mortar bombardment opened up, and we had barely hit the trench when a sausage landed on the very spot where we had been. The next few minutes were very exciting and we were kept busy dodging the sausages. We could easily see them coming through the darkness, for the fuse burned and left a trail of sparks. One would have thought they were rockets, if he hadn't seem them before. Then Fritzie opened up his artillery, and things got very warm indeed. We had several casualties, but once more our little bunch was lucky. We expected Fritzie would try to come over, so a bunch of us got out on the parapet and threw bombs and the others kept up a steady fire with their rifles. Our trench mortars were doing great work throwing over six bombs for every one Fritzie sent, and the Germans evidently thought we were too wide-awake, for they failed to show up.

Jack O'Brien

Next day I missed fourteen days' leave, and gee! I did feel sore over it. I was on sentry duty with Ernie Rowe, and I was just in the act of changing my boots for a pair of rubber waders when along came an officer. I paid no special attention to him, as a sap ran underneath Hill 60 and there were always engineering officers around. This chap stopped and passed a few commonplace remarks about the wetness of the trench, etc., and then passed on. I thought no more about it and was taking my turn at looking through the periscope, when along came Captain Breedan and a bunch of scouts. "Did you see an officer go by here?" was their excited greeting. I answered, "He went past about fifteen minutes ago. What about him?" "He's a spy, that's all, and if you had caught him it would have meant fourteen days' leave for you," said Captain Breedan. Just my luck to miss a nice fat chance like that—the beggar was never caught, he seemed to vanish into thin air. After he left me the boys kept up the hunt for a long time and then gave up in disgust.

That day I left the battalion to take a course of instruction in the Stokes trench mortar. I always had a fancy for it, as it seemed to offer a chance at getting back at Fritzie. This sitting down and taking everything he had a mind to send over, and giving nothing in return, was not my idea of fighting. I hated to leave the boys, but I was "fed up" and I wanted a change. Bink took a machine gun course at the same time and we were at the same school. When we finished he went back to the platoon and I went to the Stokes gun. The first time I went in with the gun crew, they sent us to the old St. Eloi craters. There was always lots of trench mortar fighting here, and we had orders to send over six shells for every one that came across. They put me on lookout; that is, to watch for sausages and give the boys who were working the gun time to get away. We hadn't been firing more than five minutes, and the sausages were coming thick and fast, but most of them were landing about fifty yards away, when all at once something hit me in the face. I turned around with my fists clenched, for I thought that some one had hit me. One of the boys looked at me sharply and began getting out his bandage. He said, "You're hit," then I felt the blood trickling down my cheek, and after the boys fixed me up as well as they could I went to the dressing-station. One of the boys in the trench had been killed by the shell that I got a piece of; and I was out at the dressing-station for a day or two, and then had orders to report to my unit. On my way back I met Rust and Tommy Gammon, and we sat and chatted about old times. "Come with me and join the Stokes gun," said I; "it's lots better than the infantry." "Nothing doing," said Tommy, "you're a poor advertise-ment;" and I suppose I did look funny with a big bandage around my head. "No, we are not looking for a quick funeral yet awhile," said Rust. Well, I left the boys and went on to my new unit. Some time in the next day or so Harry Foster got hit through the shoulder; and he went off looking as pleased as a dog with two tails. My, how we envied him as he walked out smoking a cigarette! But, poor chap, he died in London, and we never heard what took him off.

Shortly after this we started off for the Somme, and before we went we exchanged our Ross rifles for Lee-Enfields. We had a great time going down, we rode in cattle cars part of the way and marched the rest. Most of the roads we passed over were lined with apple trees, and gee! they did look good. When we were getting near the lines we met a division of Australians coming out from the Somme battlefield, and what sights they were! They were covered with white chalk and most of them had their trousers cut off at the knee. We asked them what it was like and they said, "Oh, you won't want a rifle, all you need is a shovel to dig yourself a hole"—cheerful, wasn't it?

Well, we went into reserves and for a couple of days we did

nothing but lounge around. We took a walk through Albert to see the statue of the Madonna and the infant Jesus. It hung right over the road, and it is marvellous how long it stayed there without being hit. The French people used to say that when it fell the war would end, but it has been down some time and the war is not over yet. They put us on fatigues and working parties for a few days and then we were moved up to the supports. We were told that we were going over the top early next morning assisted by tanks. Now, tanks had not been used up to this time and they were the surprise of the war. We hadn't heard one word about them and we were crazy to know what they were like, so our officer told us where we would find one, and away we went to see it. When we got there it was covered with a tarpaulin, but the officer in charge took the sheet off and let us have a good look: at it—and such a queer-looking monster as it was! It looked like a cross between an elephant (without his baggage) and a mud turtle. We bombarded the officer with questions, but he wouldn't answer many of them; only he said that nothing but a direct hit with a six-inch shell would penetrate its hide; and it could go through any hole or walk right over a house. It was some diabolical device all right, and we went back chuckling over the surprise that the Germans would get next day. That night we went in, marching in single file. It was pitch-dark and the Germans were shelling furiously, though before we left all our massed artillery had carried out what is known as half an hour's counter-battery work, the idea being to put as many German guns out of action as possible. Our gunners had most of the enemy positions covered, as our aeroplanes had been spotting them.

Well, we went in on the night of the 14th of September, 1916, and as I had been wounded in the knee the day before I was limping along with the other boys when, *whiz-bang*! a big shell burst right near us. It killed several of the boys that were just ahead. I hadn't been able to bend my leg a few minutes before, but believe me, I ducked when I saw that shell coming and I never thought about my knee. I was with the Stokes gun crew and was detailed off as a runner. This meant that I had to keep in touch with the various trench mortar crews, and report how things were going, to Headquarters. Tommy, Bink, and our other friends were with the battalion. Just before daybreak the Sergeant came around and gave us a snort of rum. We were lying in the trench that we had dug that night out in No Man's Land. It was called a "jumping off" trench. In front of us lay the German trench, and we were supposed to capture it and also a sugar refinery that was located a little further back. Altogether our advance was to cover about a thousand yards. Just at daybreak our barrage burst on the enemy trenches, and over we went; we got the front-line trenches without much opposition, but where the Fritzies did make a stand there was some dirty work. We were losing quite a lot of men with artillery fire. Rust was hit in the back with shrapnel, and as he half turned, a bullet caught him, smashing his jaw. Flare-pistol Bill was waving his arm to direct some of the boys when a bullet caught him in the head. But we were too busy to notice by this time, and leaving the wounded to the care of our stretcher bearers, we pushed on. We reached the second German trench and proceeded to lay out the Huns. Fat was bayoneting them as fast as he could, and "tee-hee-ing" all the time. Tommy had a big Hun in one corner, and with his bayonet under his chin was trying to make him put his hands up. At first Fritzie didn't understand, but when at last it dawned on him his hands went up in a hurry, and he cried "Kamerad!" in the approved fashion.

By this time all the Germans in sight had either been killed or taken prisoners, and a whole bunch were being herded back to our lines. The German guns were dropping heavies on the ground we had left, and as the prisoners went back they were caught in their own shell fire and a lot were killed.

From the start the tanks had been doing great work, walking over machine guns and killing hundreds with their own machine gun fire. The Germans were scared stiff and absolutely demoralized. One band, with more courage than the rest, gathered round a tank and tried to bomb it with hand grenades, but they met with no success, for the bombs either bounded off or exploded harmlessly against the steel sides. Finding their efforts useless they surrendered to the tank crew. While all this was going on, I was busy carrying messages between the gun crews and Headquarters. I was on the go all day and though the German shell fire was heavy, my luck was with me, and I didn't get hit once. Bink was dispatch runner for his company, and I passed him several times and he told me about the boys, as he was with them more than I. The last time I met him, he said, "Bob, Tommy's killed." "Tommy!" said I, almost too stunned to speak. "Yes," said he, "I was passing along the trench and had just jumped over a body when I thought the clothes looked familiar and I turned the body over, and there was poor Tommy; he had been shot through the chest by a sniper. I took charge of his things, and I'll send them to his people when I get out again." After Bink left me, I tried to realize that Tommy was gone, but I couldn't believe that my chum and bedfellow was really dead. It seemed so hard when he had only been back from hospital a few days. Well, I had no time to sit down and think, things were getting too warm.

At six o'clock that evening General Byng decided to throw in the third division, who had been held in reserve. I watched them as they came over, and it was a great sight. The 42nd Highlanders were in the lead, and they came in long lines with their bayonets fixed. The Germans spotted them as soon as they came over the ridge and immediately turned their guns on them, but they came on steadily in spite of their losses, over the top of us, and into the Hun lines. They cleaned up what was left of the Germans and established themselves firmly in Courcelette. The French Canadians had been holding Courcelette all day, but had lost heavily.

Well, that night we went back in reserve; we were all in, and we staggered along till we got to the brick fields at Albert. There we had our bivouacs and we turned in. Next morning I went over to see Bink, and we felt pretty blue. Tommy, Flare-pistol Bill, Barbed-wire Pete, and Lieutenant Oldershaw were all killed, and half a dozen others, including Rust, were wounded. Poor old 10th Platoon, they were going fast! Bink, Fat, McMurchie, Erne Rowe and I were the only ones left of my old pals, and the ones who were gone were the ones I had chummed with most. Bink and I had a lot of sad letters to write to the boys' relatives that day.

Shortly after this we were taken back of the line a few miles and reorganized, and in a few days we were back in the trenches again. The battalion went in at Courcelette a night or two before me, and such a place it was. The German artillery had made it a veritable hell-hole. What was once a pretty town was now a pile of bricks with a sunken road running through it, and leading down to a cemetery. When I went in with a Stokes gun, the 28th held the graveyard; such a time as we had getting in. We were shelled all the way, and the nearer we came to Courcelette the hotter it got. Finally we reached that sunken road and it was strewn with dead bodies, our lads and Germans. We started to set up our gun in the bank beside the road, and how we did dig. The shells were tearing up everything around us, and Tommy Lowe and I dug like demons. Our crew had three casualties almost immediately, two wounded and one killed. We got our gun set up, but as we were short of ammunition we had to wait for a counter-attack before we were allowed to fire. The 31st made an attack that morning, but got hung up on the German wire entanglements and lost heavily. When daylight came things were still hot. Sergeant Faulkner, who had just come back, after recovering from his second wound, for his final one that morning. "Carry on," he said; "I'm done." A little bunch of the 28th were holding the cemetery and expecting a counter-attack any moment. McMurchie was there in his glory. "Let the devils come," said he, "I'll chase them back with me entrinchin' tool handle." The wounded were lying around everywhere, and Tommy Lowe, Danny Dugan and I carried them up that road to the dressing-station. All forenoon the German snipers were on our track, and we had to hug the bank all the way up. The shell fire had died down, though our artillery was still giving the Germans a heavy shelling. When Tommy and I got tired we lay down in a shell hole, but the sun was hot and the odour from the dead bodies was so awful we had to move on.

That night the shelling was wicked, and we lost heavily. Our boys came along with a few prisoners, and as they couldn't get through the shell fire we allowed them to share our hole. They went out next morning, and the Huns wanted to shake hands with us for being so kind to them, but I gave one the toe of my boot and pointed the way out. Our artillery had made things unbearable for the Germans by this time, and they pulled out, leaving only a few snipers to harass us. McMurchie crawled over with a bomb and brought two of the snipers back with him. It was a funny sight to see them going up the road; those big six footers walking ahead of little Mac; the latter was barely five feet; but he marched proudly along, keeping his bayonet mighty close to them. The same day our cavalry went over, but they ran into a nest of machine guns and their little bunch was cut to pieces; it was dreadful to see the poor frightened horses running in all directions.

That night we were relieved and we went to a place called Sauage Valley. Here I said "Good-bye" to Bink; he was starting back to Blighty to get his commission. I went down the road with him and watched him till he was out of sight, and then I'm not ashamed to say that I went off into a shell hole by myself and cried like a kid. He was the last one of the old boys that had signed up with me, and now he was gone. It's hard enough to lose friends at home, but in the Army a fellow's pals are all that make life bearable. I never saw Bink again—he joined the flying corps and came down in Flanders with five bullets through his head. Well, after Binkie went, I didn't care a hang what happened. We put in another twenty-four hours in the trenches and then we started on our long march up north. We reached our destination and went into the trenches at S—. We relieved the English troops, and were there right up till Christmas. It was very quiet except for a few big raids that we pulled off; but the mud was awful. We waded through mud and water up past our waists going into the front lines, and once there we had to keep pumping all the time. Each day we would have a trench mortar scrap from two o'clock till five, and we would blow each other's trenches to pieces. I was in the trenches on Christmas day and I had two bottles of champagne that we had managed to smuggle in. I was in charge of the Stokes gun crew at that time, and I sent Tommy down to Headquarters for orders. As he left I said, "Now, Tommy, if you bring me my leave check, I'll give you five francs." After awhile Tommy came back and said, "Bob, hand out those five francs, here's your leave check." I threw him the money, and away I beat it along the trench as fast as my feet could carry me. It would have taken a "whiz-bang" to catch up to me that day. It was Xmas afternoon when I left the trenches, and the next day at 5 o'clock, still muddy and carrying my pack and rifle, I stumbled off the train at Victoria Station, and in twenty minutes I was at home, telling my old dad the tale that I have told you.

Of those ten short wild days in London I won't speak, but it was like getting to heaven after being in hell. They slipped by much too quickly, and then the time came for me to go back. So one morning I landed up at Victoria Station and caught what is known as "the train of tears." The boys are always very silent going back—there is never any cheering. After you have had eighteen months of hell, war is not the grand romantic thing it seemed at first. The boys feel as if they were on their way to a funeral, and the worst of it is, it may be their own. But once in France, every one seems to brighten up again, and the game goes on as before. Memories of home die away, and you become simply an atom in the big war machine. It took me some time to get settled down again, and they kept moving us in and out of the trenches. It was terribly wet and cold, and we would sit for days all huddled around our old charcoal brazier in a dugout forty feet under ground. Of course a dugout at this depth was comparatively safe. Only once did Fritz blow in the entrance with a trench mortar, and then we had to dig ourselves out. After about two weeks longer the whole division went out on rest. At least, they called it "rest," but our time was kept so filled up with drilling, inspections, etc., that we got "fed up" and wished we were back in the lines. We had about a month of this, and then we went in and took over our new positions at the Labyrinth to the right of the Ridge. The Labyrinth was a perfect maze of trenches, built by the Germans, and taken from them by the French, at the time of the British attack at Loos. The gun crew we relieved was carried out in sandbags, having been blown to pieces by a premature shell—that is, a shell exploding in the gun. This made us pretty nervous, and we didn't fire any more till all our stock of ammunition had been inspected. After our second trip in on this line, we went out and commenced our training for the Battle of Vimy Ridge. We were taken back to a piece of country that was much like the district we would have to fight on. It was all blocked off with different-coloured tapes representing towns, trenches, and various other landmarks, and for two weeks we had to go over this ground, in the time and manner of a real attack. I, being a Stokes gunner, had to go with my gun and crew, and we had four guns behind each battalion. Our work was to set up our gun as quickly as possible and drop bombs on any machine gun that happened to be holding up the infantry. The infantry went over in waves—one wave would take a trench and hold it till the next wave went over their heads, and the next wave went over them again, and so on. After a couple of weeks of this we went into the trenches at the spot from which our advance would start; this was to make us familiar with the ground. We spent seven days here, and during this time our guns were put into position in pits, in No Man's Land. These pits were covered with wire netting woven in and out with grass to hide us from the observation balloons. Our artillery were keeping up a ceaseless bombardment of the enemy's lines, destroying and obliterating the German trenches. At the same time our long-distance guns were firing night and day on all roads, towns, and ammunition dumps that lay near the enemy's lines, while our aeroplanes were over the Germans all the time. But our aircraft was having hard luck, for the Huns had just brought out a new lot of planes and these were lighter and faster than ours. It was heart-breaking to see our air men being shot down. I have seen six or seven of our planes come down in one day. Up to this time our planes had reigned supreme, and the hostile airmen scarcely dared to show themselves; and even now the Hun's triumph was short-lived. Our Colonel insisted that the newest planes be brought over, and when they came we had the satisfaction of seeing the Huns cleaned up. Well, after a week in the trenches we were taken out and given a real rest. We were allowed to lie around pretty much all the time, while the boys in the trenches kept the Germans on the jump. Every night they would go over and destroy the enemy's dugouts and bring back a bunch of prisoners; from these prisoners they got a lot of valuable information.

All this time the roads leading to our lines were packed night and day with men, transports, guns, ammunition, limbers, and everything that is needed for a big charge. Our eighteen-pound guns were in long lines, wheel to wheel. Behind them were long lines of heavier guns and back of these a line of long range naval guns. These last fired six- and twelve-inch shells to a distance of fifteen miles at targets given them by aeroplanes. The enemy artillery shelled our roads a little, but whenever they started, our guns would redouble their efforts and the ground was shaking with their roar day and night.

The evening before the big attack our artillery carried out counter-battery work, destroying as many as possible of the enemy's guns. Just at dusk we fell in line and began our march to the trenches. We passed through St. Eloi (not the one in Belgium) and the French people looked at us pityingly. They didn't think it possible for us to capture Vimy Ridge, where the French troops had lost thousands in a vain attempt the year before. Our artillery fire had died down and the night was quiet when we marched into our assembly trenches at Neuville St. Vaast. The Stokes gun that I was with and one other were detailed to go over with the last wave of the 27th Battalion. That meant that we would have to go the farthest. Everything was quiet, and Tommy and I lay down in the trench and covered ourselves with our water-proof sheets and went to sleep. We slept till the officer came along with our rum. Then we watched the front line, and our watches; all at once, with a roar, our artillery burst forth. It is impossible to describe the sound, the earth shook with it, and it was like a thousand thunderclaps, continually rolling, and for miles along the enemy's trenches a sheet of flame was dropping as our liquid-fire shells fell in a ceaseless rain. For awhile the Germans shot their S.O.S. flares, but these soon died down.

The German artillery was slow in retaliation, and before they got properly started our first brigade had taken the first line of trenches, and our fifth brigade was over the top of them and pressing forward. They followed our barrage as it advanced so many yards at a time, destroying all opposition. Soon the 4th and 5th Brigades had attained their objectives with few casualties and our officer told us to get ready, so the "Iron Sixth" started to move. When the first three battalions had gone, the 27th went over, and we jumped out, shouldering our guns and advancing in file. We hadn't gone more than a couple of hundred yards when gas shells began to come. On went our masks, but hardly in time—we got a couple of whiffs. Two of the boys had to go back to the dressing-station, but the rest of us had to go on. We were feeling mighty sick but when we got to where the air was clear, we took off our gas helmets and we felt a little better. We soon forgot our ills in the excitement of the charge, as we went on over what had been the German front line, but now was manned by our men. The pioneers were already pushing forward a light railway, and our aeroplanes were fighting overhead. By the way, the Royal Naval triplanes had been sent over 'specially for this work, and they did great execution among the enemy planes. We pressed on till we caught up with our barrage. The German shell fire was very erratic, the guns seemed to be firing anywhere; on our right and left stretched long lines of smoke as the British advanced, but our flanks were not coming up fast enough, and we had to wait; meanwhile our barrage played on a wide belt of barbed wire that was just in front of us. Some of our men got too close to the barrage and were hit by our own shells.

At last the barrage lifted, and the 27th and 28th went through the belt of wire, cutting with the attachments on their rifles, any strands that our artillery had failed to sever. A machine gun commenced firing at us, so down our crew went into a shell hole and up went our gun and a few rounds silenced that machine gun; then forward again with the 27th. We struck a trench and worked our way down, for this was our objective. On the way we came to a large dugout, and it was full of Germans. As soon as we appeared at the entrance they started to holler, and one man tried to get out the other entrance, so our Sergeant shot him. We took the rest of them prisoners (about twenty altogether, officers and men) and we lined them up and went through their pockets. We took away their revolvers, badges, photos, and all sorts of things—in fact, we stripped them of everything but their lives and a few clothes and sent them back to our lines.

We set up our gun in the trench and waited for a counter-attack. While we were waiting we regaled ourselves on the good things we had found in the dugout; black bread, bottles of wine, and cigars. Tommy and I had to stay out on the gun, and pretty soon the German heavies began to shell the trench, and we had to dig ourselves in to protect us from the shrapnel. To make things more comfortable, it commenced to rain and all that night it poured. We were right on the crest of the Ridge and a number of the boys were hit carrying messages back to Headquarters. When morning came we found that our position overlooked miles of the enemy's country. We could look down on green fields and little villages, and close to the bottom of the hill lay the railway and the little town of Tarbus.

The boys had turned the German guns around and were firing at the retreating Huns. Some of the guns we had captured were in big concrete emplacements with six feet of concrete and steel on top of them. They were still hot from firing when our boys took them and our crews with them. The Germans gave up very easily, and I don't wonder, for our artillery fire had demoralized them. One of our men had a German belt, and on the buckle were the words "Gott mit Uns" or "God with Us," but they must have a different God from ours if they expect help from Him after the deeds they have done.

That night, after Tommy and I had taken our turn on the gun, we went down into the dugout and made some tea. Tommy lay down on the floor, but the only space I could find was on a bench beside a dead German; but I slept just as soundly as I would have in a feather bed. The next day about noon our officer came and said, "Well, boys, we've got to go over again, and a dirty job we are in for too." Then he told us that at three o'clock we had to be down and have our guns set to fire on a tower in Farbus where a number of snipers were located. We had to go in advance of our outposts and stay there till our boys were ready to attack. About two o'clock we started out—our gun crew and a party carrying bags of ammunition. Little Robbie, a boy who had joined up with me at Moose Jaw, turned to me and said, "Well, Bob, this is where I get mine, and I hope I'll get it right through the bean—life's no pleasure to me." "Aw, cheer up," said I; "you may get a nice Blighty." "No," said he; "I belong to a bunch that get it good and hard when it comes at all." Poor Robbie!—he had lost all of his chums at Hooge, and he seemed to know that his time had come. He got separated from us when we were going down the hill, and he went to one of our other guns. They told him where we were, and he started to walk across the open and he got shot right through the head. Meanwhile we had sneaked forward, taking advantage of a little flurry of snow, and we got as close to Farbus as we dared to go. We set up our guns and at the appointed time opened fire. The 27th had started down behind us, but the Germans saw them and opened up, and they must have had the place packed with machine guns, for a stream of lead swept over our heads. The attacking party were almost wiped out; our officer had crawled up ahead and was signalling us the range and how many rounds to fire. Tommy and I were lying flat and working the gun. The officer saw that the attack was a failure, and he came back to us and said, "Well, boys, we got down here—now the thing is to get back. We'll take our time and make use of all the cover we can find." So, shouldering our gun, away we went, the officer leading. We started to climb the Ridge, and we were just coming through a churchyard when *rat-a-tat-tat*! a machine gun spoke to us from the town we had left. The Corporal jumped and fell, and when we reached him he said, "Boys, I've got it." We bound him up as best we could, and Tommy went in search of a stretcher to carry him out on. But while he was gone, we tried to get the Corporal to walk a little way. He was shot through the groin, and he wouldn't move no matter how we coaxed. So the Sergeant and I got rough, and said, "Now, look here, you've got to walk; if you don't, we will go away and leave you here to die." This brought him to his senses, and leaning on our shoulders he went forward slowly till we found the road, and then the going was easier up to the top of the Ridge. When we reached the top the shelling was awful, so we put the Corporal on a concrete gun pit, and when Tommy and the stretcher arrived we carried him back to Thelner.

That night we were relieved, and utterly exhausted we stumbled our way back through the shell fire to Neuville St. Vaast. Once there, we got some hot grub from our cooks and a big drink of rum, and we turned into our dugouts, but now that the strain was over I couldn't sleep and I shook like a leaf. Tommy was beside me and he said, "Quit your shaking, you son of a gun; I do my shaking in the line, but you do yours after we get out." Next day we went still farther back and we were allowed a week's complete rest, and in the meantime our line was advanced to Arleaux.

When we were returned to the lines we were told that it was over the top again for us; the Canadians were going to make an attack on Fresnoy. The town of Fresnoy was only a short distance from Arleaux, which we now held, and about one mile from Vimy Ridge. The ridge it was on made it important as an observation post, and through the town ran a line of trenches known as the Oppy switch of the Hindenburg Line. To the 1st Division was given the task of taking the town, while the 2nd Division attacked the trenches on the left.

We went in during the night when it was fairly quiet, and we took over the gun positions, from a trench mortar crew. Just before daybreak our barrage burst on the enemy and away we went and got in close to their wire entanglements. As soon as the barrage lifted, through the wire we went and into the trench, but instead of a wave of infantry being in with us they got hung up on the wire and lost heavily; so half a dozen of our crew were in the trench by ourselves. The Germans were only too willing to be made prisoners at first, and threw away their rifles, but when they saw that no one else was coming they got fresh and started to bomb us. Our Corporal was shooting them as fast as he could with his revolver and we dropped our gun and pelted them with their own bombs. We managed to chase them back along the trench and the 1st Division sent us help, so we blocked the trench and held over part of it. Our boys on the left had also gotten in and cleared out a section of the trench, so it was a sandwich with the Germans for our meat. We were relieved that night, but only stayed out long enough to get a rest and some food, and next night we were back again. The shelling was dreadful when we were going in and we had to keep on the run all the way up—and carrying guns, that was no joke. Every road we crossed had a heavy barrage put on it and we had a lively time. We had almost reached the front lines when one of our officers got hit in the face by a piece of "whiz-bang." Well, finally we got in and we spent all the next day sniping Germans as they tried to run across the open to get to another trench. One Hun got lost and walked almost up to our section of the trench before he found out his mistake; he tried to go back, but a bullet chipped by him and he came in and gave himself up. Tommy and I were on lookout when we were surprised to see a German crawl to the edge of our trench. I was just going to fire, when Tommy said, "Wait a minute," and he danced around and stuck his bayonet up under the German's nose; up went the hands, and we hauled the wretch in. He was wounded in the leg; we gave him a drink though water was very scarce, we only had one bottle among three; then we gave him a kick and sent him on his way rejoicing back to his lines.

The third night we were relieved—shelling had been heavy all day and all the approaches to our lines were blotted out—the barrages had made them impassable during the day. I was sent out to act as guide to the relieving party, and I found them sitting down under a heavy barrage. They had been shelled all the way from Vimy and were so "all in" that they didn't care what happened. After much persuasion I got them to come along, and finally we reached our line, and we went out leaving them in possession of the trench. We were scarcely out of sight when the Germans counter-attacked, and the crew we had just left were wiped out. Three times the German penetrated parts of the line and three times they were thrown back. Our casualty list was very heavy. Fresnoy fell into their hands again in spite of the fierce resistance our boys put up.

In the meantime we got through the barrage all right, though we lost some of our men. A shell dropped just ahead and blew the man in front of me to pieces; I got his body all over me and I was blood and dirt from head to foot. But we kept on going till some one ran out of the darkness shouting, "You cannot get past the railway, Fritzie has been throwing over gas shells and the gas is thick in the valley, all our artillery is gassed." We put on our masks, but we couldn't see through them very well and we decided to hang out where we were till morning, but Fritzie began sending us some high-explosive shrapnel and we thought we would rather take our chance with the gas, so we stuck our gas tubes in our mouths, grabbed our noses, and away we went. The Germans were flinging heavy shells at our silent artillery, but we got past all right and we stumbled on till we came to our camp at Neuville St. Vaast. One or two had been gassed a little and had to go to a dressing-station, but the rest of us had a good feed and we went right to sleep—we sure were "all in." We only did one more trip into that part of the line, and then it was very quiet, so to our great joy we were taken out and given a month's rest.

The next time we went in was at Lens, and here we relieved some British troops that had been having an awful time. They were holding a place on the outskirts of Lens known as Cite Ste. Elisabeth, and they told us some awful tales of what had been taking place. The British had attacked Lens, but after being practically successful the attacking party were not able to hold what they had gained. The Germans surrounded the town, and those that were not killed were taken prisoner. Now, Lens was merely a mass of ruined houses, but the Huns had fortified every house and were firmly intrenched. The troops we relieved were holding what had been German territory, and they had made fortresses out of the houses that were still standing. They had lost half their men, and it was marvellous what they had done and the way they had held out.

The gun position that our two Stokes guns took over was in a big house, or rather behind it. The basement of this house was propped up with mine timbers and steel props; this was to sustain the eight feet of concrete with reinforced steel that had been laid on the first floor. It made a wonderful protection for our guns and also for ourselves. The basement

　　　　Jack O'Brien

contained box spring-beds and real mirrors, and we felt that we were very swell indeed. We kept most of our ammunition in the house, where it was always dry, and the way we hammered old Fritz wasn't slow. We fired from two to three hundred rounds daily and our carrying parties cussed us for firing so much. When not on the guns we spent our time in the basement telling yarns and playing cards. We had a dandy officer; he had only just come out, but he was as keen as mustard. He insisted on living with us, and when we were firing he was right on the spot. Of course with our gun going so much of the time Fritzie came back with everything he had, but he never could find out where we really were. The greatest drawback to our new position was the lack of water. Before the Germans retired they had filled all the wells with barbed wire. The Germans tried to gas us out, and sometimes they would pelt us with gas shells; all night long we had to sleep with our gas masks on. On the whole, our position here was much better than what we were used to, and we thoroughly enjoyed it, but after we had been here for a few days we were taken out on rest and then sent to another place.

This time we went in at Liever, and our positions here were hellish. I don't know how we lived through it; we were there four days, and in that time our guns were either blown up or buried at least twice a day. One night Tommy and I were lying in a hole that we had dug right beside our gun, and without letting us know, our fellows in the trenches sent over a cloud of gas. The Germans always bombarded where gas was sent over, and this was no exception to the rule. They started at once. Tommy and I were lying in the most exposed part of the trench and Tommy was snoring, when with a crash the shells began bursting over us. I wakened Tommy, for one gets so that he sleeps through everything, and we lay there wondering what would happen next. Suddenly, *bang*! a shell hit the side of the hole we were in and filled the hole with smoke and covered us with dirt. I said, "Come on, Tommy, let's go down the trench a bit where it isn't so blamed hot." "Naw," says Tommy, "it's a long chance on him hitting us again." The words were hardly out of his mouth, when crash came another shell and it buried us in dirt this time. We were just scrambling out and Tommy was ahead, when *bang*! another shell landed right in front of us. Tommy went still and I grabbed him. "Tommy, Tommy, have they got you, kid?" No answer, and I shook him again; he squirmed and started to swear, and I knew that he was all right. We scrambled out and were beating it down the trench when an officer came out of a dugout and asked us what was the matter. We told him and he said, "What size were the shells that came over?" "Huh," said Tommy, "they was comin' too damned fast for me to measure 'em." The officer grinned, and we went on. At the end of four days we were relieved and sent back on rest.

After a few days they sent us back to Lens, and there was something doing every minute there this time. Our artillery was steadily bombarding the enemy's lines, and our boys were putting on raids almost every night. When a raid was being made our guns would throw bombs on either side of the sector attacked to prevent reinforcements coming up from the sides, then our artillery would put up a barrage behind the front line to keep back help from the supports, thus hemming them in on three sides with shell fire while our infantry attacked from the front. A great many prisoners were taken in this way, but our losses were very light. Not long after this, on August the 18th, the 1st Division of Canadians made their big attack on Hill 70. At the same time our boys made an attack on the outskirts of Lens. The attack was a complete success, though afterwards the Germans made five successive counter-attacks and our losses were heavy. The slaughter in these counter-attacks was awful. I was in the reserve trenches at the time watching the prisoners and the wounded streaming past. Half of our Stokes gun battery was in reserve, and the other half in the firing-line. About noon the day after the first attack was made, word came out that one of our crew had caught it and asking for help and stretchers to carry out the wounded. So we made our way in through a perfect inferno and we found the crew—an officer and six men—all lying wounded in a dugout. We got busy and carried them out, and poor beggars, they got some awful bumps as we stumbled along through the darkness, over dead bodies and through shell holes. We had just passed safely through the barrage when gas shells came over and we had to put masks on the wounded as well as on ourselves. We got them all to the dressing-station, but one of the boys died just after we got them in. Poor Roy Taylor—he was marked for leave the next day.

The following night we went in again with our guns and our boys were billed for another attack. The gun I had charge of was supporting the 29th Battalion, while behind us in the trenches lay the 28th. My orders were to open fire at the same time that the artillery did, about 4 A.M., and my job was to blow out a blocked trench that led up to the German lines. This was to enable our boys to advance without losing many men. After doing this I was to keep on firing well in advance of our troops till I reached the limit of my range, and then go up the trench and place the gun in a spot that would cover a point from which a counter-attack might be expected. These were my orders, and I was given five men to help manage the gun. The Stokes gun will fire one hundred twelve-pound shells in three minutes, if no time is lost with misfires. It takes two men to work the gun and one to hand up ammunition. I sent three men down the trench to be ready in case of need and the other two helped me. Exactly on the dot the artillery and our gun opened up, and for five minutes there was just the banging and flashing of explosives all around. The Germans opened up their artillery and attacked at the same minute that our boys went over—and it was a real hell. Of course I couldn't see what was going on—around us there was nothing but explosions and smoke. My three spare men were hit, but so far we had escaped. Some Germans were behind us, having worked their way around from the left, but we didn't know it. Finally one of the boys said, "Just five more shells, Bobby," so I said, "All right, we'll save them, come along, and we'll pick out a new place for our gun." So, away we stumbled up the trench, half blinded by smoke and the concussion of the exploding shells. As we went on in the trench leading to the German lines I began to wonder what had happened—dead Germans were lying in heaps—but we kept on, thinking that our attacking party were away ahead, when all at once we ran into a bunch of "square-heads." They were on the outside of the trench as well as the inside, and then started the damnedest scrap I was ever in. Two of the boys were armed with rifle and bayonet, and I had a revolver. We shot those Fritzies just as fast as they stood up, and then they lay down and threw hand grenades at us. How we killed all those in the trench I don't know, things are hazy in my mind. Faces came and went, and it's like a horrible dream. The old fellow beside me gave a yell and dropped, hit in the back by a piece of one of the exploding grenades. I was out of ammunition and I flung my revolver at the nearest Fritzie, and thinks I, "It's all up now, and I don't care a d—anyway." I tried to drag the old man into a dugout and I got him on the stairs, but he looked so bad that I laid him down and started cutting away at his tunic to find the wound. The Germans that were left started firing bombs at me, but they went over my head and down the stairs bursting on a pile of wounded below. All at once, one hit the roof of the dugout and dropped at my feet. It exploded and it was just as if some one had thrown a bucket of boiling water all over my legs. I put down my hand and my leg was full of holes and the blood was literally streaming from it. The pain was awful and I couldn't stand up any longer. I was half fainting, and I dropped into the dugout on a pile of writing bodies. But I still had sense enough to know that if I stayed there the next bomb that came down those stairs would land on my back, so I managed to scramble off, and then I crawled along the dugout floor till I came to a table. It was black dark and I had to feel my way along. I pulled myself up on the table and started to bind up my leg, when along came one of our crew, Benson; he had bayoneted the man who was throwing bombs, and had come into the dugout by the other entrance. He helped me fix myself up and along came one of our own stretcher bearers. We called to him and he told us that the old 28th had come to our rescue and had chased the Germans out of the trench. The stretcher bearer was working like a hero, sorting out the wounded, binding them up and getting them ready to move. My old man had managed to get downstairs and he was calling, "Bobbie, Bobbie, come and help me." I told him that I couldn't go, for I was hit myself. The stretcher bearer lit some candles and we had a look around; one entrance of the dugout was blocked and the dead were lying everywhere. Benson did his best to make me comfortable, but the bone was sticking out through the side of my leg and it was mighty sore. After awhile an officer of the 28th came down and said, "Sorry, boys, but we've got to drop back; the Germans are attacking heavily, and we are not strong enough to hold them here, we will have to leave you, but if you are here we will come back for you tomorrow morning." We groaned. I tried my best to get up the stairs, but after two or three attempts I had to give up. Benson had to go to help the boys hold the Fritzies in the next line of trenches. After awhile along came the Germans—the stretcher bearer saw them as they passed the entrance. In the dugout we all kept as still as we could. There were thirty of us, all badly wounded, and caught like rats in a trap.

The Germans did not bother coming down, but they threw

bombs in every time they passed. These bombs killed a number of the boys and the smoke and gas almost choked the rest of us. This continued all day and all night. An Irishman with a leg and an arm broken was lying at my side; and he just lay there grinding his teeth and cursing the Germans. Just after daybreak we heard a lot of bombs bursting in the trench above and we wondered what was happening. Soon we heard a footstep on the stairs and some one shouted, "Who's down there!" and one of our sergeants appeared with a bomb in his hand. "It's us!" we cried, and perhaps we were not glad to see him! He said, "All right, boys, we'll get some stretcher bearers up and have you taken out as soon as possible." In about half an hour along came a carrying party; they took the Irishman up just ahead of me, and I could hear him grinding his teeth. Gee! but that fellow had grit. We had just gone a little way down the trench when *bing*! one of the stretcher bearers got a bullet through the top of his tin hat. It didn't touch, but it came too close for comfort and they kept pretty low after that. As they carried me along some one passed me on the run going out, and I called "Hello, Benson." He turned around and, gee! he was glad to see me alive. He grabbed one end of the stretcher and insisted on helping to carry me out, so away we went to the advance dressing-station. I had to wait my turn, for there was a long line of wounded. "Well, Bobbie, what shall I do?" asked Benson. "Go back and report to Headquarters," I said. "And, by the way, Benson, what happened to our gun?" "Oh," said he, "a shell landed right on top of it and blew it to smithereens." Not long after old Tucker came along and said, "Got a Blighty, Bob?" "Yes," says I, "and I'll be lucky if I don't lose my leg." By this time my leg was swollen up like a balloon, and I was afraid of blood poisoning. When at last my turn came at this dressing-station they just gave me an injection to prevent poisoning and sent me on. After much jolting in a motor ambulance I arrived at a big clearing-station and had my leg properly dressed. Then they put me

Jack O'Brien

aboard a Red Cross train, and I was lying there feeling pretty tough when a sweet voice said, "Would you like a cigarette?" I opened my eyes, and there stood a Red Cross nurse. Say, she looked like an angel to me. I guess the other boys felt the same, for their eyes followed her wherever she went. Just before daylight we arrived at the little town of Camiens, and we were tenderly carried off the train and put into motor ambulances. The road was very rough, and at every jolt we would all swear. Then, to our amazement, a lady's voice said, "I'm sorry, boys, but the road is rough." I looked up and there, driving the ambulance, was a young lady. Gee! we did feel ashamed. Finally we arrived at our destination and were carried into a big base hospital. It was an American hospital, and it sure seemed like heaven after what we had been through. They soon fixed up my leg, and then I had nothing to do but watch the nurses. They were the most efficient doctors and nurses I ever saw; everything in the hospital moved like clockwork. After a few days they set my leg and put it in splints and then I waited for my ticket to Blighty; but my troubles were not quite over. One day the German aeroplanes came over, and next night they came again and bombed our hospital. Oh, it was awful—worse than the front lines. They dropped six bombs, killed a doctor, wounded some nurses, and killed and wounded many of the boys. I lay in bed hanging onto the pillows and listened to the crash of the bombs, and the screams of the wounded. I hope I will never hear the like again. One of the bombs came through the tent I was in, but didn't explode. The minute the Huns were gone the doctors and nurses were around looking after the boys, soothing those who were shaken and attending the ones who were injured. There was no excuse for the bombing of this hospital; it was plainly marked with the Red Cross, and no one could mistake it for an ammunition dump. A few days more, and I was shipped across to dear old Blighty and three months of heaven. It was worth all I had gone through to be treated as we all were over there. I was in several hospitals, and it was the same in all—they were just as good to us as our own people could have been. The X-ray showed fifty-six pieces of tin in my leg. As the doctor remarked, "You are a regular mine, and I think we will let you take your fifty pieces back to Canada; it would destroy too many nerves to dig them out, and in time they will work up to the surface."

So, here I am back in Canada, a civilian with fifty-six pieces of iron in my leg to remind me that I spent Two Years in Hell.

Your chum,
BOB.

THE RED, RED ROAD TO HOOGE

You're on parade, go get your spade,
Fall in, the shovel and pick brigade,
There's a carry fatigue, for half a league,
And work to do with the spade.
Through the dust and ruins of Ypres town
The seventeen-inch still battering down,
Spewing death with its fiery breath,
On the red, red road to Hooge.

Who is the one whose time has come,
Who won't return when the work is done,
Who'll leave his bones on the blood-stained stones
Of the red, red road to Hooge?
To the sandbagged trenches and over the top,
Over the top if a packet you stop
On the red, red road to Hooge.

The burst and roar of the hand grenade
Welcome us to the "death parade,"
The bit of gloom and valley of doom,
The crater down at Hooge.
Full many a soldier from the Rhine
Must sleep tonight in a bed of lime—
'Tis a pitiless grave for brave and knave,
Is the crater down at Hooge.

Hark to the "stand-to" fusillade,
Sling your rifles, go get your spade,
And spade away ere the break of day,
Or a hole you'll fill at Hooge.
Call the roll, and another name
Is sent to swell the roll of fame,
So we carve a cross to mark a loss,
Of a chum who fell at Hooge.

Not a deed for a paper man to write,
No glorious charge in the dawning light,
The "Daily Mail" won't tell the tale
Of the night work out at Hooge.
But our General knows, and his praise we've won,
He's pleased with the work the Canadians have done,
In shot and shell at the mouth of hell,
On the red, red road to Hooge.

Jack O'Brien

"THE IRON SIXTH"

(6th Brigade, 2nd Canadians, 27th, 28th, 29th, and 31st Battalions)

Canada's Golden Gateway sent forth her gallant sons,
Who proudly marched with smile and song to face the German guns;
Where'er their duty called them 'twas there they won their fame,
And on the Scroll of Honour is the "TWENTY-SEVENTH'S" name.

Yet farther west, and still her sons is Canada sending out:
The "TWENTY-EIGHTH" Battalion fights with never a fear or doubt;
From the head of Lake Superior and the Province of Golden Wheat
The boys are marching 'gainst the foe with never falt'ring feet.

B. C. has sent her quota, and the "TWENTY-NINTH" is there,
Broad-chested, stalwart manhood, just out to do and dare;
Vancouver's boys are marching with steady step and true,
Determined all to play the game and see the whole thing through.

A breath from Calgary's city, flung where the fight is worst—
Still more of Canada's manhood is the gallant "THIRTY-FIRST."
From prairieland and city they answered to the call,
And bravely shouldered rifle lest their Empire's honour fall.

From Winnipeg's Golden Gateway to Vancouver's rainy shore,
Come Canada's sons to keep the flag of Empire to the fore;
From Kemmil down to Ypres, go when and where you will,
The "IRON SIXTH" have paid their toll, and are bravely paying still.

Canada, O Canada! the Pride of all the West,
We'll fight for thee, we'll die for thee, so that our Homeland be
The Bounteous land, the glorious land,
Forever of the free.

WALTER T. H. GRIPPE.

28th (N.W.) Battalion,

June 12th, 1916.

Choose from Thousands of 1stWorldLibrary Classics By

A. M. Barnard
Ada Leverson
Adolphus William Ward
Aesop
Agatha Christie
Alexander Aaronsohn
Alexander Kielland
Alexandre Dumas
Alfred Gatty
Alfred Ollivant
Alice Duer Miller
Alice Turner Curtis
Alice Dunbar
Allen Chapman
Alleyne Ireland
Ambrose Bierce
Amelia E. Barr
Amory H. Bradford
Andrew Lang
Andrew McFarland Davis
Andy Adams
Angela Brazil
Anna Alice Chapin
Anna Sewell
Annie Besant
Annie Hamilton Donnell
Annie Payson Call
Annie Roe Carr
Annonaymous
Anton Chekhov
Archibald Lee Fletcher
Arnold Bennett
Arthur C. Benson
Arthur Conan Doyle
Arthur M. Winfield
Arthur Ransome
Arthur Schnitzler
Arthur Train
Atticus
B.H. Baden-Powell
B. M. Bower
B. C. Chatterjee
Baroness Emmuska Orczy
Baroness Orczy
Basil King
Bayard Taylor
Ben Macomber
Bertha Muzzy Bower
Bjornstjerne Bjornson

Booth Tarkington
Boyd Cable
Bram Stoker
C. Collodi
C. E. Orr
C. M. Ingleby
Carolyn Wells
Catherine Parr Traill
Charles A. Eastman
Charles Amory Beach
Charles Dickens
Charles Dudley Warner
Charles Farrar Browne
Charles Ives
Charles Kingsley
Charles Klein
Charles Hanson Towne
Charles Lathrop Pack
Charles Romyn Dake
Charles Whibley
Charles Willing Beale
Charlotte M. Braeme
Charlotte M. Yonge
Charlotte Perkins Stetson
Clair W. Hayes
Clarence Day Jr.
Clarence E. Mulford
Clemence Housman
Confucius
Coningsby Dawson
Cornelis DeWitt Wilcox
Cyril Burleigh
D. H. Lawrence
Daniel Defoe
David Garnett
Dinah Craik
Don Carlos Janes
Donald Keyhoe
Dorothy Kilner
Dougan Clark
Douglas Fairbanks
E. Nesbit
E. P. Roe
E. Phillips Oppenheim
E. S. Brooks
Earl Barnes
Edgar Rice Burroughs
Edith Van Dyne
Edith Wharton

Edward Everett Hale
Edward J. O'Biren
Edward S. Ellis
Edwin L. Arnold
Eleanor Atkins
Eleanor Hallowell Abbott
Eliot Gregory
Elizabeth Gaskell
Elizabeth McCracken
Elizabeth Von Arnim
Ellem Key
Emerson Hough
Emilie F. Carlen
Emily Bronte
Emily Dickinson
Enid Bagnold
Enilor Macartney Lane
Erasmus W. Jones
Ernie Howard Pie
Ethel May Dell
Ethel Turner
Ethel Watts Mumford
Eugene Sue
Eugenie Foa
Eugene Wood
Eustace Hale Ball
Evelyn Everett-green
Everard Cotes
F. H. Cheley
F. J. Cross
F. Marion Crawford
Fannie E. Newberry
Federick Austin Ogg
Ferdinand Ossendowski
Fergus Hume
Florence A. Kilpatrick
Fremont B. Deering
Francis Bacon
Francis Darwin
Frances Hodgson Burnett
Frances Parkinson Keyes
Frank Gee Patchin
Frank Harris
Frank Jewett Mather
Frank L. Packard
Frank V. Webster
Frederic Stewart Isham
Frederick Trevor Hill
Frederick Winslow Taylor

Friedrich Kerst
Friedrich Nietzsche
Fyodor Dostoyevsky
G.A. Henty
G.K. Chesterton
Gabrielle E. Jackson
Garrett P. Serviss
Gaston Leroux
George A. Warren
George Ade
Geroge Bernard Shaw
George Cary Eggleston
George Durston
George Ebers
George Eliot
George Gissing
George MacDonald
George Meredith
George Orwell
George Sylvester Viereck
George Tucker
George W. Cable
George Wharton James
Gertrude Atherton
Gordon Casserly
Grace E. King
Grace Gallatin
Grace Greenwood
Grant Allen
Guillermo A. Sherwell
Gulielma Zollinger
Gustav Flaubert
H. A. Cody
H. B. Irving
H.C. Bailey
H. G. Wells
H. H. Munro
H. Irving Hancock
H. R. Naylor
H. Rider Haggard
H. W. C. Davis
Haldeman Julius
Hall Caine
Hamilton Wright Mabie
Hans Christian Andersen
Harold Avery
Harold McGrath
Harriet Beecher Stowe
Harry Castlemon
Harry Coghill
Harry Houidini

Hayden Carruth
Helent Hunt Jackson
Helen Nicolay
Hendrik Conscience
Hendy David Thoreau
Henri Barbusse
Henrik Ibsen
Henry Adams
Henry Ford
Henry Frost
Henry James
Henry Jones Ford
Henry Seton Merriman
Henry W Longfellow
Herbert A. Giles
Herbert Carter
Herbert N. Casson
Herman Hesse
Hildegard G. Frey
Homer
Honore De Balzac
Horace B. Day
Horace Walpole
Horatio Alger Jr.
Howard Pyle
Howard R. Garis
Hugh Lofting
Hugh Walpole
Humphry Ward
Ian Maclaren
Inez Haynes Gillmore
Irving Bacheller
Isabel Cecilia Williams
Isabel Hornibrook
Israel Abrahams
Ivan Turgenev
J.G.Austin
J. Henri Fabre
J. M. Barrie
J. M. Walsh
J. Macdonald Oxley
J. R. Miller
J. S. Fletcher
J. S. Knowles
J. Storer Clouston
J. W. Duffield
Jack London
Jacob Abbott
James Allen
James Andrews
James Baldwin

James Branch Cabell
James DeMille
James Joyce
James Lane Allen
James Lane Allen
James Oliver Curwood
James Oppenheim
James Otis
James R. Driscoll
Jane Abbott
Jane Austen
Jane L. Stewart
Janet Aldridge
Jens Peter Jacobsen
Jerome K. Jerome
Jessie Graham Flower
John Buchan
John Burroughs
John Cournos
John F. Kennedy
John Gay
John Glasworthy
John Habberton
John Joy Bell
John Kendrick Bangs
John Milton
John Philip Sousa
John Taintor Foote
Jonas Lauritz Idemil Lie
Jonathan Swift
Joseph A. Altsheler
Joseph Carey
Joseph Conrad
Joseph E. Badger Jr
Joseph Hergesheimer
Joseph Jacobs
Jules Vernes
Julian Hawthrone
Julie A Lippmann
Justin Huntly McCarthy
Kakuzo Okakura
Karle Wilson Baker
Kate Chopin
Kenneth Grahame
Kenneth McGaffey
Kate Langley Bosher
Kate Langley Bosher
Katherine Cecil Thurston
Katherine Stokes
L. A. Abbot
L. T. Meade

L. Frank Baum
Latta Griswold
Laura Dent Crane
Laura Lee Hope
Laurence Housman
Lawrence Beasley
Leo Tolstoy
Leonid Andreyev
Lewis Carroll
Lewis Sperry Chafer
Lilian Bell
Lloyd Osbourne
Louis Hughes
Louis Joseph Vance
Louis Tracy
Louisa May Alcott
Lucy Fitch Perkins
Lucy Maud Montgomery
Luther Benson
Lydia Miller Middleton
Lyndon Orr
M. Corvus
M. H. Adams
Margaret E. Sangster
Margret Howth
Margaret Vandercook
Margaret W. Hungerford
Margret Penrose
Maria Edgeworth
Maria Thompson Daviess
Mariano Azuela
Marion Polk Angellotti
Mark Overton
Mark Twain
Mary Austin
Mary Catherine Crowley
Mary Cole
Mary Hastings Bradley
Mary Roberts Rinehart
Mary Rowlandson
M. Wollstonecraft Shelley
Maud Lindsay
Max Beerbohm
Myra Kelly
Nathaniel Hawthrone
Nicolo Machiavelli
O. F. Walton
Oscar Wilde

Owen Johnson
P.G. Wodehouse
Paul and Mabel Thorne
Paul G. Tomlinson
Paul Severing
Percy Brebner
Percy Keese Fitzhugh
Peter B. Kyne
Plato
Quincy Allen
R. Derby Holmes
R. L. Stevenson
R. S. Ball
Rabindranath Tagore
Rahul Alvares
Ralph Bonehill
Ralph Henry Barbour
Ralph Victor
Ralph Waldo Emmerson
Rene Descartes
Ray Cummings
Rex Beach
Rex E. Beach
Richard Harding Davis
Richard Jefferies
Richard Le Gallienne
Robert Barr
Robert Frost
Robert Gordon Anderson
Robert L. Drake
Robert Lansing
Robert Lynd
Robert Michael Ballantyne
Robert W. Chambers
Rosa Nouchette Carey
Rudyard Kipling
Saint Augustine
Samuel B. Allison
Samuel Hopkins Adams
Sarah Bernhardt
Sarah C. Hallowell
Selma Lagerlof
Sherwood Anderson
Sigmund Freud
Standish O'Grady
Stanley Weyman
Stella Benson
Stella M. Francis

Stephen Crane
Stewart Edward White
Stijn Streuvels
Swami Abhedananda
Swami Parmananda
T. S. Ackland
T. S. Arthur
The Princess Der Ling
Thomas A. Janvier
Thomas A Kempis
Thomas Anderton
Thomas Bailey Aldrich
Thomas Bulfinch
Thomas De Quincey
Thomas Dixon
Thomas H. Huxley
Thomas Hardy
Thomas More
Thornton W. Burgess
U. S. Grant
Upton Sinclair
Valentine Williams
Various Authors
Vaughan Kester
Victor Appleton
Victor G. Durham
Victoria Cross
Virginia Woolf
Wadsworth Camp
Walter Camp
Walter Scott
Washington Irving
Wilbur Lawton
Wilkie Collins
Willa Cather
Willard F. Baker
William Dean Howells
William le Queux
W. Makepeace Thackeray
William W. Walter
William Shakespeare
Winston Churchill
Yei Theodora Ozaki
Yogi Ramacharaka
Young E. Allison
Zane Grey